CFBaker.
W9-DDG-636

Buffalo Architecture: A Guide

Buffalo Architecture: A Guide

Introductions by
Reyner Banham
Charles Beveridge
Henry-Russell Hitchcock

Text by
Francis R. Kowsky
Mark Goldman
Austin Fox
John D. Randall
Jack Quinan
Teresa Lasher

Sponsored by the Buffalo Architectural Guidebook Corporation

The MIT Press
Cambridge, Massachusetts
and London, England

Inclusion of a building in this guidebook does not imply right of entry.

Disabled people may obtain information from the Advocacy Office for People with Handicapping Conditions, 1602 City Hall, Buffalo, New York 14202

Third printing, April 1982
Second printing, January 1982
© 1981 by The Massachusetts Institute of Technology

All rights reserved. No part of this book may be reproduced in any form or by any means, electronic or mechanical, including photocopying, recording, or by any information storage and retrieval system, without permission in writing from the publisher.

This book was set in Compugraphic Univers by A & B Typesetters and printed and bound by Halliday Lithograph in the United States of America.

Library of Congress Cataloging in Publication Data

Main entry under title:
Buffalo architecture.

Bibliography: p.
Includes index.
1. Buffalo (N.Y.)—Buildings—Guidebooks. 2. Architecture—New York (State)—Buffalo—Guidebooks. I. Banham, Reyner.
NA735.B83B83
917.47'970443 81-4476
AACR2
ISBN 0-262-52063-X (paper)
ISBN 0-262-02172-2 (hard)

Frontispiece:
Architectural detail, Old Post Office, Buffalo

Contents

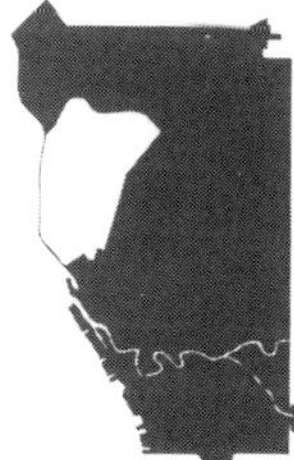

3
Black Rock
and Riverside
172

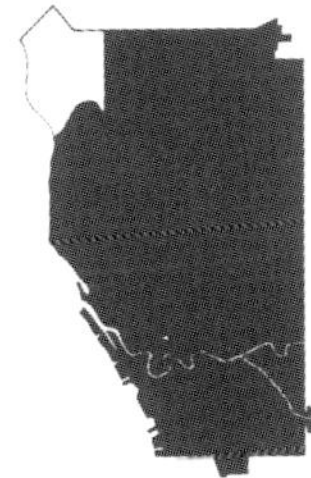

4
North Park
and Central
Park
188

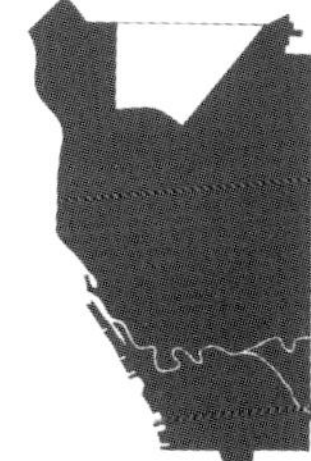

5
Kensington-
Bailey
211

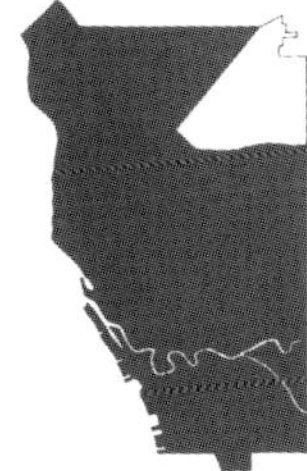

6
East Side
224

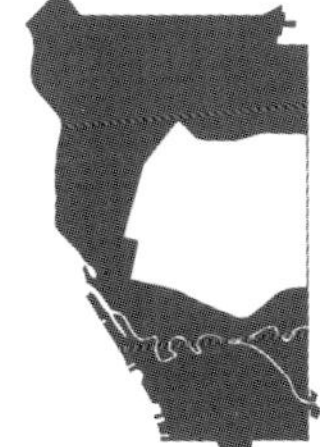

Acknowledgments

The directors and officers of the Buffalo Architectural Guidebook Corporation gratefully acknowledge contributions from the following foundations and organizations. These contributions provided the major funding that enabled the guidebook to move from an idea to a reality.

American Institute of Architects, Buffalo-Western New York Chapter

Baird Foundation

Cameron Baird Foundation

Coopers & Lybrand

Peter C. Cornell Trust

Delaware North Companies

Fisher Foundation

Fletcher Paper Company

Graphic Controls Corporation

Junior League of Buffalo, Inc.

Seymour H. Knox Foundation

Landmark Society of the Niagara Frontier

Margaret L. Wendt Foundation

Society of Architectural Historians, Western New York Chapter

Stritt and Priebe, Inc.

Western New York Foundation

The Guidebook also is made possible, in part, with public funds from the New York State Council on the Arts.

Many more people than the directors of the corporation, listed below, have contributed significantly to the work involved in publication. Three people deserve special mention: Edwin T. Bean, Jane F. Clemens, and Rose M. Sury.

With warmth, appreciation, and sincerity, we thank those named and unnamed, including private donors, for what they have done. We hope that the guidebook will be worthy of their efforts.

Directors and Officers of the Buffalo Architectural Guidebook Corporation

Stanley Arbeit (Associate Professor of Marketing, Canisius College); Jason P. Aronoff (School Psychologist, Kenmore—Town of Tonawanda Schools); Mary Banham, 1979–1980 (artist, art educator); Kathryn E. Carroll, Secretary (M.Arch., State University of New York at Buffalo); William M. E. Clarkson, Chairman and President (Chairman and Chief Executive Officer, Graphic Controls Corporation); Robert Traynham Coles, Vice-President (FAIA; Director, Buffalo–Western New York Chapter, AIA); Richard B. Dopkins, Treasurer (Partner, Magavern, Magavern, Lowe, Beilewich, Dopkins and Fadale); Austin M. Fox, Vice-President (Former President, Landmark Society of the Niagara Frontier); Francis R. Kowsky, 1980– (Professor of Fine Arts, State University College at Buffalo); Thomas D. Mahoney (Owner, Mahoney and Weekly Book Sellers); Richard E. Moot (Senior Partner, Damon, Morey, Sawyer and Moot); Steven A. Nash, 1979–1980 (Assistant Director/Chief Curator, Dallas Museum of Fine Arts); Mitchell Owen, 1979–1980 (Administrative Vice-President, Buffalo Sabres); John D. Randall (Director, The Architectural Museum and Resource Center); Lenore Rubin (Codirector, More-Rubin Art Gallery); John S. Sprague (President, Sports Surfaces and Structures, Inc.)

Preface

The City of Buffalo is an outdoor museum of extraordinary architecture, developed over the one hundred fifty years of its history. Its buildings and public spaces are among the best in the country, yet its place in American architecture has seldom been recognized. This guidebook is intended to acquaint both residents and visitors with the city's architectural treasures. It focuses on existing buildings, although some of the outstanding architectural works that Buffalo has lost are described in a brief chapter.

This is a book about buildings; it is also a book about Buffalo, about architecture in its historical, geographical, and sociological context. Thus, while concentrating on the city, it extends to the areas on both sides of the Niagara River that have traditionally been associated with the life of Buffalo: the eight Western New York counties, including Erie and Niagara, as well as Southern Ontario, Canada.

In spite of the strength of Buffalo's architectural tradition, it was not until the late 1970s that a combination of interested and capable people came together to produce a guidebook. Among them were Jason Aronoff, architectural enthusiast, who recognized the need for such a publication; Jack Randall, architect and preservationist, who wrote and produced the definitive *Buffalo and Western New York: Architecture and Human Values* (1976); Mary Banham, catalyst and first coordinator of the Buffalo Architectural Guidebook Corporation; Kate Carroll, second coordinator and indefatigable worker; and Reyner Banham, architectural historian, author, educator, and critic.

Organizations that acted as prime movers were the Landmark Society of the Niagara Frontier and the Western New York Chapter of the Society of Architectural Historians. Finally, there was the Buffalo Architectural Guidebook Corporation, created to put the concept together, develop the funding, and bring the work to finished form and into publication.

Architecture is a public act and so should be of interest to everyone; furthermore, it helps determine an area's quality of life. If people want a great city, they must not only act to preserve good buildings, but must also set standards for new ones. The opportunity lies in finding the resources and in liberating our ideas, our imagination, and the desire for excellence. So, to know what we have today is one of the best ways to envision what we could have in the future.

Those of us who have helped bring this guidebook about hope that it will contribute to the appreciation and preservation of our architectural heritage, while we work on creating the Buffalo of the future.

William M. E. Clarkson
President and Chairman
Buffalo Architectural Guidebook Corporation

Buffalo Architecture: A Guide

Introduction

Reyner Banham

This book is intended to make it impossible, ever again, for anyone who cares about architecture to say, "We drove by Buffalo on the Thruway, but decided not to stop because there's nothing there to look at—is there?"

Anybody who knows enough of architecture to care about it will already know that two of the world's most celebrated office buildings were built here: Adler and Sullivan's Guaranty Building of 1896, and Frank Lloyd Wright's Larkin Administration Building almost a decade later—and if the Larkin has been gone for over thirty years, the Guaranty (under its later guise as the Prudential) is with us still, after many vicissitudes, to remind us of Buffalo's golden age of architecture.

And it does not stand alone. Great buildings do not occur in isolation; they grow out of flourishing architectural cultures where the habits of good construction and imaginative planning have solidity and momentum. To underline this point, the Prudential stands in an urban context which, though shredded by dubious "improvements" of the last two decades, still retains fragments and survivors to remind us how solid the tradition of good building was hereabouts.

In front of the Prudential is St. Paul's Episcopal Cathedral, Richard Upjohn at his picturesque Gothic best, its red Medina sandstone and spiky silhouette elegantly contrasted against the paler terra-cotta regularity of Sullivan's vertical pilasters and flat roofline. Across Main Street stands the vast, off-white city block of

Church Street, showing the Prudential Building, the Ellicott Square Building, the old Post Office, and St. Paul's Cathedral

D. H. Burnham and Company's Ellicott Square Building, the same age as the Prudential and the largest office building in the world at the time of its completion. Although it has lost its cornice, it retains its great glazed courtyard inside, covered by a glass roof larger than that of Burnham and Root's Rookery Building in Chicago, and—unlike the Rookery's blacked-out glazing—still transparent to the summer sun, which streams over its elaborate mosaic floor.

These samples remind us of the quality of the downtown that was, but quality was not restricted to the central business district. The history of Buffalo and of its planning ensured that good buildings would be located at many points, or would even cover whole districts, distributed all over the area now incorporated in the City of Buffalo.

The city was built not upon one good plan, but three, responding to its statistical growth, the movements of its wealth and people, and its civic ambitions. The first plan, the Black Rock plan, laid down a simple grid of streets to serve the mile-wide strip of government lands along the east bank of the Niagara River. That grid made sense for the original riverside community, but for that very reason was turned almost at 45 degrees to the cardinal north-south/east-west orientation that made better sense for the lands behind the riparian strip.

So, when Joseph Ellicott—brother of Pierre L'Enfant's assistant in the laying out of Washington, D.C.—came to parcel out in 1797 the enormous tract of land that had been purchased by the Holland Land Company, he was faced with the tricky problem of meshing two grids that could not be meshed. His solution to the problem of relating the Black Rock grid to the layout of most of the rest of Western New York was a neat geometrical maneuver: to create a plaza from which eight streets, radiating at equal angles, fed into both grids. That plaza is now known as Niagara Square, the civic heart of the Buffalo metropolis, dominated by the astonishing Art Deco bulk of City Hall (1929–1931) by Dietel, Wade and Jones, and focused on the prim needle of the monument to President McKinley at the center. Yet this resolved the problem at only one nodal point, however important, and left, for more than half a century of the city's growth, an uneasy seam of unresolved junctions straggling for miles to the north. It is

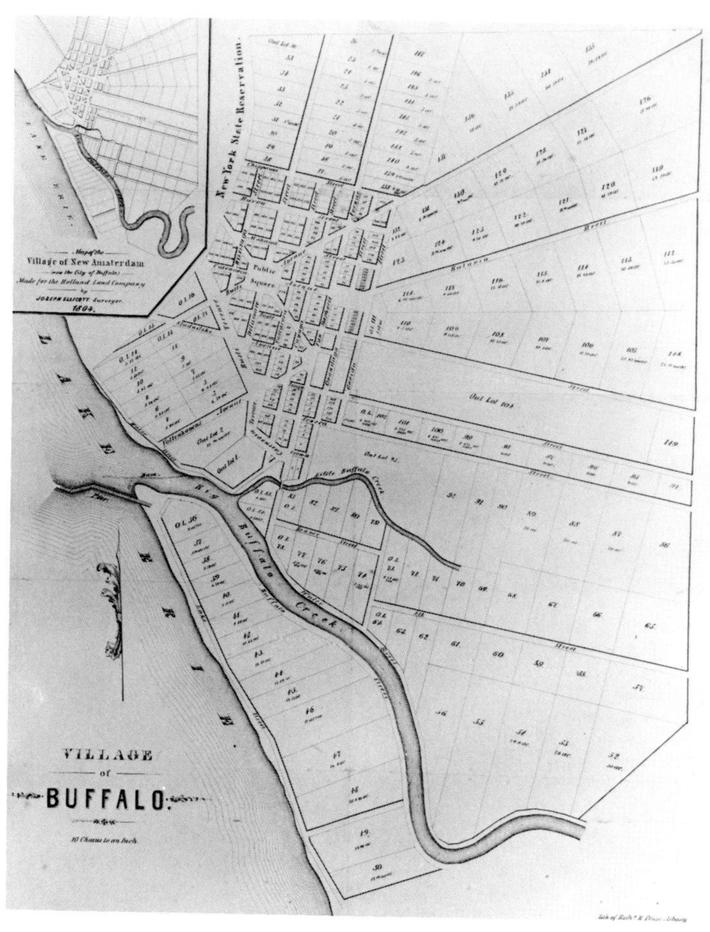

Plan for the Village of Buffalo, by Joseph Ellicott, 1804

still there—represented by the dotted line of the reservation boundary—in maps from as late as the 1860s, but after that the northern part, from North Street to West Ferry, disappears, resolved at the behest of a gardener, not a city planner.

That part of the unresolved seam became, instead, Richmond Avenue, one of the most important links in the chain of parks and parkways devised by Frederick Law Olmsted at the very end of the 1860s. Yet Olmsted did more than this. In a plan now internationally recognized as ranking with Baron Haussmann's slightly earlier replanning of Paris (and sometimes called its "democratic equivalent") Olmsted gave shape and coherence to a city that was about to launch on a phase of spectacular growth.

He drew a thin line of green up from the bank of the Niagara River to Symphony Circle—now the site of the Saarinens' Kleinhans Music Hall as well as of the tall campanile of First Presbyterian Church by Green and Wicks—then north along Richmond Avenue to the circles and parkways of the upper West Side. There, with a broader brush, he laid in the green acres of the grounds around H. H. Richardson's Buffalo State Hospital, and Delaware Park, which embowers the neoclassical niceties of the Historical Society Building (all that survives on the 1901 Pan-American Exposition site) and the Albright Art Gallery (with Gordon Bunshaft's "Knox" addition). The third green swath that completes this great scheme (by inclusion, since it already existed) is Forest Lawn Cemetery—known to all lovers of Victorian monumental eccentricity as the location of the enthralling and appalling Blocher tomb.

This tall loop of green ways and green places gave order to a city in the process of creating itself out of disjointed subdivisions and opportunistic industrial installations. Unlike so many grandiose schemes, Olmsted's does not divide communities or frustrate growth; craftily threaded through undeveloped land and disregarded landscape opportunities, it defined boundaries and discovered character.

Both were needed; transportation was beginning to impose on Buffalo the same kind of ruthless transformations that it wrought on all other nineteenth century cities. Black Rock and Buffalo had grown up close to the lake, along the rivers and the Erie Canal, which opened in 1825, but from 1845 onward the railroads were shifting the components of the city around the surface of the map. Olmsted's plan held the center together, and its influence extended beyond the grounds contained within the loop, defining the new, preferred areas for residential building.

Thus, the plan directly created the site for one of the five houses of world stature by Frank Lloyd Wright that grace the Buffalo scene, Soldiers Place, which provides the greenery in front of the big porch of the Heath house. But the influence of the plan extends northeast into the Parkside area—designed by Olmsted though executed differently—and beyond, and thus also gave the sites for the classic Martin house and its outliers, the Barton house and the gardener's cottage, and further afield still, the site for the Davidson house, on Tillinghast Place.

Now, these five works of America's greatest domestic architect raise two topics of crucial importance in understanding the quality of Buffalo architecture; first, all were built for members of the Martin connection, the administrative "cadre" who ran Buffalo's most prodigious industrial builder, the Larkin Company, in its most impressive years; second, they were the final seal of excellence set upon a remarkable body of residential architecture and planning, so important for the city that it demands immediate attention.

To take this second point first: No visitor who passes beyond the most superficial acquaintance with Buffalo fails to comment on the quality and quantity of the housing surviving from before 1914, and its concentration in areas of conspicuous desirability. Such areas penetrate even now into the western parts of downtown—as at Johnson Park with its central green surviving, albeit truncated by Elmwood Avenue, and in the rest of West Village behind. An area of small streets full of neat and fanciful small houses lies on the south-facing slope between Allen and North Streets; and beyond North Street, which was once the "frontier" of the city, there extends a broad band of high-quality residential streets, lying between Richmond Avenue on the west and Delaware Avenue, traditional address of the mightiest mansions of the extremely rich, on the east. This prestigious zone of domesticity extends northward to the confines of Delaware Park, and even overleaps it in places, since Nottingham and Middlesex avenues on one side, and Parkside on the other, are manifestly part of the same system of development.

Pockets of quality housing have survived throughout the rest of the West Side too, and, in spite of cataclysmic physical, economic, and social changes, even to the east of Main Street. Indeed, lucky accidents—or are they?—such as the stability of ethnic working-class communities have sustained the environmental quality of clusters of residential streets lost among factories and switching yards in strange and unexpected areas, such as Milburn or Monroe Street in the "deep east" or between the Church of the Assumption on Amherst Street and the industrial strip created by the Belt Line Railroad three blocks north. The houses may not be great architecture but the residential charm of these well-maintained little streets is undeniable.

All sorts and conditions of men built these Buffalo houses. In the 1860s and 1870s German carpenters built elaborately crafted dwellings for their own occupation, and as speculations, in the East Side area now known as the Fruit Belt (after its street names), while powerful magnates commissioned the three mansions by McKim, Mead and White—the Butler and Pratt houses and the earlier Metcalfe house, which was demolished in 1980—at Delaware and North, or the Dorsheimer house, by H. H. Richardson, that stands farther south on Delaware. Between these extremes of the modest and the palatial, and the third point of reference given by Frank Lloyd Wright's domestic innovations, almost every possibility of nineteenth-century domestic architecture was explored in Buffalo.

Nearly all of it was uncommonly well made; late Victorian housing in the area is admired and treasured for its glass—the clear, etched and bevel-cut, even more than the stained and colored—and for its woodwork. Buffalo is a city where elaborate carving in native and exotic woods abounds, reaching some kind of apotheosis in the more formal interiors of buildings such as the Connecticut Street Armory. The style of a great deal of this woodwork may not please all modern tastes, but it carries the conviction of the dedicated workmanship that went into it, and of the fat, bustling merchant society that commissioned it.

Houses on Bridgeman Street in Black Rock
Doorway, Richmond Avenue

Stairway, Connecticut Street Armory

One does not look for craftsmanship of this type or quality in Wright's houses, however. They belong to another world—the wide world of the twentieth century, the Machine Age. He himself pointed out that *his* moldings were built up from the "plain, machine-cut rails . . . that the machine can render far better than would be possible by hand"; and his clientele were men of a new age: managers, salaried executives, who saw themselves in various ways differently from the entrepreneurs who had built Buffalo's wealth and monuments in the previous century.

Nowhere was this different vision more manifest than in the Larkin Administration Building that Darwin Martin commissioned from Wright. Almost certainly the first "front-office" building in North America, it emphasized the new power of management, its separation from the processes of manufacture, not only in its proud and monumental forms, but in its location, on the opposite side of Seneca Street from Larkin's factories and warehouses. It was a monument of change, the tombstone of one epoch in Buffalo's economic and human history, the point of departure for a second phase so different from the first in its topography and energies that it is hard to compare the one with the other.

In world terms, the most important buildings which initiated that new age were probably the workshops of the Buffalo Forge Company on Broadway, for it was here that Willis Haviland Carrier did most of the fundamental research and development that made air conditioning a commercial possibility, and thus permanently altered the relationship between buildings and their external environment. In Buffalo terms, however, it is buildings connected with transportation and electricity that mark the changes still, even if the official commemoration of that change, the Tower of Light at the Pan-American Exposition, survives only in a pale echo in the cresting of the Niagara Mohawk tower at Washington and Genesee.

It was the opening of the Belt Line Railroad in 1883 that was fundamental to these changes. Together with cheap hydroelectric power from Niagara Falls in the nineties, it made it possible to spatter factories and other facilities anywhere along a wide suburban ring without reference to the water that had been the traditional source of power, or the carrier of fuel. Buffalo's most glamorous contributions to the new transportation age are located hard by the Belt Line and far from the traditional industrial locations on the harbor; the Pierce-Arrow factory on Elmwood Avenue, a complex to which national talents as consequential as those of Albert Kahn of Detroit and Lockwood, Greene & Company of Boston contributed, and the Pierce-Arrow showroom (now the Braun Cadillac dealership) on Main Street—appropriately enough, opposite the entrance to Jewett Parkway, which leads directly to Wright's Martin house.

Farther along Main Street, near the next set of railroad bridges, stands a decidedly Bostonian building of even greater elegance and structural innovation, also by Lockwood, Greene, built for the Buffalo Meter Company. It is now the university's Bethune Hall, named after the first woman architect to practice in the United States, Louise Blanchard Bethune, a member of the Buffalo firm which designed the downtown Lafayette Hotel.

Now, this is but a short listing, a sampling, from a remarkable crop of high-quality industrial buildings that come from the transitional phase of Buffalo industry—say, 1890 to 1920—which is also the golden age of Buffalo's industrial architecture. In the Larkin Company's numerous surviving buildings—and they dwarfed the missing Administration Building in both height and bulk—one can see every phase of the structural, as well as organizational, transition in industry, from almost undifferentiated work space built in massive "regular mill construction," to the highly specialized warehousing, elegantly realized in reinforced concrete (again by the Lockwood, Greene & Company), and packaged into the enormous terminal warehouse now occupied by Graphic Controls.

By a kind of economic freak, and in some ways a sad one, Buffalo also retains a rare and noble set of another kind of transitional industrial buildings—grain elevators. While it is true that Buffalo is the place where the operating principles of the grain elevator were invented (in 1842, by Joseph Dart), none of the wooden structures that first embodied those principles lasted very long because of frequent fires. Conversely, it is true that the type of grain elevator most familiar to us today, with its ranks of concrete cylinders, is not native to Buffalo, but came from Minneapolis after 1900.

In the late 1890s, however, Buffalo acquired two historically important intermediate elevators with steel bins—the Great Northern, now part of the Pillsbury Mills; and the Electric, the first to be powered by electricity. Both still survive, as do two of the earliest concrete type, which are of historical importance because they were, through another freak circumstance, well known in Europe. These were the Washburn-Crosby, now General Mills, close by the Skyway, and Concrete Central, now abandoned in solitary and desolate grandeur on an inaccessible site along the Buffalo River. Through frequent photographic illustration in European publications they may have done almost as much as the Buffalo works of Wright and Sullivan to shape the progress of modern architecture world-wide. Walter Gropius knew these photographs, as did Le Corbusier. Erich Mendelsohn was the first of many pilgrims to come to Buffalo to see for himself.

But to modern architecture as such, Buffalo contributed little directly in the way of buildings. Like many another North American city it lived out the 1920s under the spell of late eclectic classicism and of Art Deco—quite apart from the large works in that mode, such as City Hall, and the Central Terminal on Memorial Drive (and minor ones like Harold Plumer's Pierce-Arrow showroom), Main Street downtown boasted other choice examples, of which the Courier-Express Building by Monks and Johnson still survives, with its sculptured and back-lit terra-cotta facade.

Beyond this, architecture, and building generally, in Buffalo faltered in the 1930s and 1940s except for industrial and—once again—automotive work, such as the Chevrolet plant on the city's northern fringe, by Albert Kahn and noted world-wide as a model of its kind. And since then, revival has been slow: the cluster of business towers downtown, the University's Amherst campus out of town, have brought some distinguished architectural signatures to Buffalo, but their effect on the city has hardly been galvanic, nor their style especially Buffalonian.

The way ahead is obscure; the city needs new buildings for economic and functional reasons, but psychologically it also needs new buildings of high architectural quality, if it is to regain the habits of good building. The new bus terminal by

Larkin Company, 1924
Grain elevators on the Buffalo River

Cannon Design fulfills all three criteria; but there is an added element of passion—or, at least, personal vision—about two smaller recent downtown buildings: the steel box of studios for WKBW/Channel 7, an "energy-responsible" design by Stieglitz Stieglitz Tries, and the same team's Naval and Servicemen's Park building, sitting pretty under the Skyway, against the looming silhouettes of the USS *Little Rock* and its partner-in-retirement, *The Sullivans*. Locally designed for special local needs, these buildings seem the most promising pointers for an architectural recovery in Buffalo.

Yet anyone, local or outsider, who comes here to build nowadays, must know that the quality of the work can—and will—be measured by tough standards. Whether they offer to build an office block on a downtown street, a hotel by the water, a factory by the tracks, or a house on a suburban green, they have only to look around to see that mighty ghosts observe their work—Richardson, Sullivan, Burnham, Wright, Upjohn or Stanford White, Albert Kahn or the impeccable Lockwood, Greene—and the monuments from their ancestral drawing boards still cast long shadows across the sites where anyone else would build in the Queen City of the Lakes. The context of quality, however eroded, is still physically present, still inspiring, and still very demanding on the conscience of anyone who knows enough of architecture to care about it.

Buffalo's Park and Parkway System

Charles Beveridge

The Buffalo park and parkway system, designed between 1868 and 1898 by Frederick Law Olmsted and his firm, has a special place in the history of American city planning. The first stage of the system, designed by Olmsted and his partner, Calvert Vaux, and carried out between 1868 and 1876, is particularly important. It was the first of many such systems planned by Olmsted and his successors and was the first demonstration of the form he hoped the expanding American city would take.

The focus of the Olmsted-Vaux system was 350-acre Delaware Park, called simply "The Park" in the original plans. It was the only public space designed by Olmsted in Buffalo that met his definition of the term "park"—a setting of pastoral scenery extensive enough to provide complete escape from the artificiality and noise of the city. It was also the first park for which Olmsted selected the site. The design that he and Vaux prepared was a classic one, consisting of a 243-acre upland "meadow park" of greensward and scattered trees that was separated by Delaware Avenue (then Delaware Street) from a sheltered "water park" containing a 46-acre lake that was formed by damming Scajaquada Creek.

In order to keep the traffic on Delaware Avenue from disturbing the peaceful atmosphere of the park, the designers used a technique they had developed with the sunken transverse roads crossing Central Park. They ran the street below the surface of the park where they could, hid it with thick plantings, and planned the paths and drives in the park so that they crossed over it on

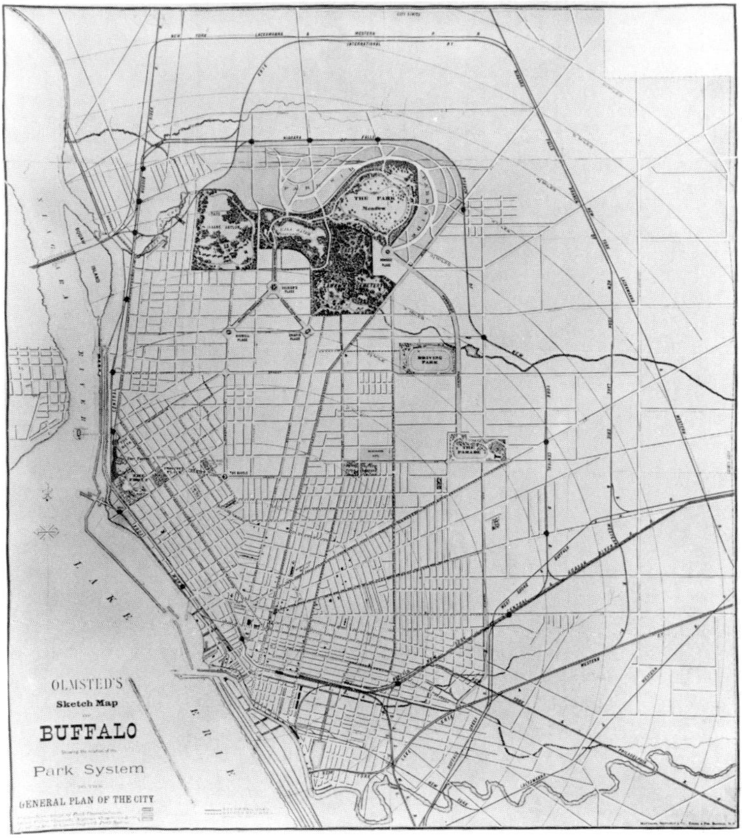

Plan for the Buffalo park system, by Frederick Law Olmsted, 1874

Delaware Park, the Lake and the Casino, circa 1900

a single bridge. Olmsted and Vaux also provided for complete separation of pedestrian and vehicular traffic, so that the danger of collision would not distract visitors from relaxed enjoyment of the scenery. The expressway that now runs through the midst of the park along the course of one of the old carriage drives provides a melancholy contrast with the careful way in which Olmsted and Vaux planned for the movement of traffic.

The 120-acre meadow, now a golf course, is still one of Olmsted's finest open spaces, and the thick stand of trees outside the circuit drive illustrates the way he "planted out" the city beyond. The zoo and its parking lot have expanded to fill an area originally used as a fenced meadow for deer. In the corner of the park near Agassiz Circle there were several abandoned quarries; they were transformed into a series of landscaped pools, following designs made by the Olmsted firm in 1898. They have since been filled, and the only remnant of the 1898 designs is a balustraded bridge, now level with the lawn.

Olmsted and Vaux included two other public grounds in their system: the 56-acre Parade (now Martin Luther King, Jr., Park) and the 32-acre Front. They designed these places for activities that would have been incongruous and distracting to the quiet enjoyment of rural scenery for which alone they created the Park. The Front, on the Erie Canal near its entrance to Lake Erie, served as a formal waterside gateway to the city. It had a carriage concourse, bandstand, playground, and amphitheater. Today expressways and the approaches to the Peace Bridge intrude on the Front and obstruct the view over the lake, but the playground and concourse are more or less intact.

The Parade, on high ground to the east, provided a view over the city and lake, and contained a parade ground, a grove full of play equipment for children, and a large refectory designed by Calvert Vaux. In 1896 the Olmsted firm redesigned the area, replacing the playground with a picnic grove and introducing, on the site of the parade ground, a series of geometric water features that included a shallow circular basin over five hundred feet in diameter, a rectangular basin for aquatic plants, and a circular fountain area. Today a hockey rink and tennis courts occupy the sites of the two latter features. The science museum, constructed in 1929, occupies much of what was once the spacious entrance of Humboldt Parkway.

The final element of the plan by Olmsted and Vaux for Buffalo was a series of wide, shaded parkways and streets that connected the Park, Front, and Parade with each other and with the rest of the city. The designers also intended these parkways and streets to serve the need for open space of the neighborhoods through which they passed. As Olmsted described what he hoped to achieve:

Thus, at no great distance from any point of the town, a pleasure ground will have been provided for, suitable for a short stroll, for a playground for children and an airing ground for invalids, and a route of access to the large common park of the whole city, of such a character that most of the steps on the way to it would be taken in the midst of a scene of sylvan beauty, and with the sounds and sights of the ordinary town business, if not wholly shut out, removed to some distance and placed in obscurity. The way itself would thus be more park-like than town-like.

The major streets leading to the Park were Delaware Avenue, connecting Niagara Square with Gates Circle, and Richmond Avenue, connecting at Ferry and Symphony circles with streets running to the Front, and joining the parkways at Colonial Circle. The parkways had 200-foot rights of way, along which ran walks and roads and from six to eight rows of trees. On the west side they began at Gates Circle. and Colonial Circle and converged at Soldiers Place to form Lincoln Parkway, which ran north to the Park. On the east side, Humboldt Parkway connected the Park with the Parade. Both Lincoln and Humboldt parkways had the special feature devised by Olmsted and Vaux that distinguished their parkways from earlier avenues and boulevards: a central, smoothly paved road for the sole use of private carriages. This carriage drive was flanked on each side by a median with trees, grass, and walks, outside of which were streets for carts and wagons. The four parkways connecting to Delaware Park were the first parkways constructed according to plans made by Olmsted and Vaux. A final link in the Buffalo system was Fillmore Avenue, running south from the Parade.

The Dutch elm disease of recent years has taken a heavy toll on Buffalo's parkways, but current replanting programs promise to restore the West Side parkways and access streets to something like their old attractiveness. On the east, however, Humboldt Parkway has been demolished by Kensington Expressway.

Olmsted grafted his parkway system onto the original radial street plan of Joseph Ellicott, and believed that the combination made Buffalo "the best planned city, as to its streets, public places and grounds, in the United States. . . ." He drew up a map of the city showing these elements, proudly displayed it at the Centennial Exposition in Philadelphia in 1876, and won an honorable mention with it at the Paris Exposition of 1878.

After the end of his partnership with Calvert Vaux in 1872, Olmsted continued to design Buffalo's public spaces. In 1874 he made a new design for Niagara Square, and during the next two years he planned the grounds of the new city and county building (now Old County Hall).

A hiatus of over a decade followed, and when Olmsted returned to Buffalo in 1887 he proposed to create a park and parkway system in South Buffalo that would solve the basic problems of drainage and transportation facing the city in that section. He prepared a design for a 240-acre park on Lake Erie at the city line, consisting primarily of winding waterways between islands to be formed by dredging the marshy site. His plan provided for boating and other activities that stimulated "gayety, liveliness, and a slight spirit of adventure." On the inland side of a railroad embankment next to the park he proposed to have a rifle range that would be flooded in winter for skating. Provision in this place for active sports would, Olmsted hoped, forestall any attempt to intrude them into the quiet scenery of Delaware Park.

The parkway system running out from the proposed south park was to serve as part of a larger scheme for planning the growth of the southern part of the city. The parkways would run through local neighborhoods and then join at a grand viaduct over the broad belt of railroad tracks in the vicinity of the Buffalo River, securing safe and pleasant access to the rest of the city. At the same time the marshy areas on the south side would be drained, and the dike

Bidwell Parkway, circa 1930

created along the lake for the purpose would make possible a four-mile promenade and carriage drive to the south park and a sheltered canal for access to it by boat.

The city fathers rejected Olmsted's proposal as too costly and asked him instead to make designs for two low-lying inland sites that he found "too large for local grounds, too narrow and cut up for parks." His designs for South Park and Cazenovia Park, therefore, were attempts to create passages of scenery in limited spaces while providing at the same time for a variety of recreational needs. His design of 1894 for 155-acre South Park combined pastoral scenery of greensward, groves, and water with an arrangement of 2300 species of trees and shrubs for use as an arboretum. There was also provision for a large conservatory building. Many species still survive, and the waterside scenery, especially on the islands in the lake, give the effect of picturesque richness, variety, and profusion that Olmsted desired. In that respect, South Park provides a telling contrast with the barren shores of the Delaware Park lake.

In his design for 76-acre Cazenovia Park, Olmsted provided for local activities with a playground, carriage concourse, and picnic grove that are still in use. He also sought to secure some of the boating and skating activities that had been the highlight of his first South Park design. He proposed to dam Cazenovia Creek with a removable structure that would permit boating during part of the year and also lower the water level for safe skating in the winter. At the same time he created a passage of water scenery, with islands, inlets, and thickly planted shores. The islands and inlets have now been filled in, and the shallow creek runs a direct course through the park. Since the realization of Olmsted's plan, one hundred and ten acres have been added to the park upstream, primarily for a golf course.

The parkway system designed by Olmsted for South Buffalo consists of McKinley Parkway, running from South Park to Heacock Place at the intersection of South Park Avenue and Abbott Road, and connecting at McClellan Circle with the short spur of Red Jacket Parkway that runs to Cazenovia Park. Olmsted's hope for a grand parkway-viaduct connecting the two sections of his system was not realized.

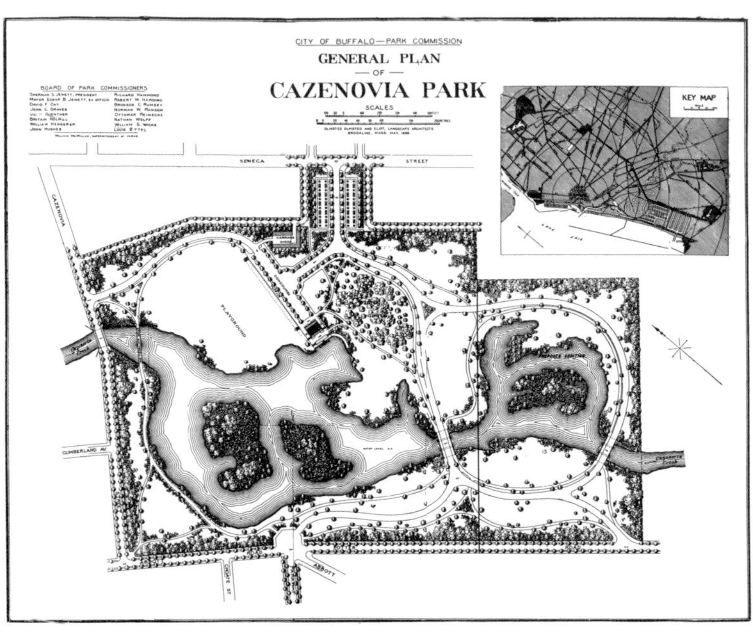

Plan, Cazenovia Park, Olmsted, Olmsted and Eliot, 1896

Cazenovia Park

The last public ground designed in Buffalo by the Olmsted firm was Riverside Park, on the Niagara River in the northwestern part of the city. In 1898, three years after Olmsted's retirement, the firm presented a plan for the 22-acre site. Its features included a fountain, music court, and several buildings, arranged on an axis toward the river and extending on a footbridge over the Erie Canal to a boat landing and pergola on the river. A *Y*-shaped curvilinear road system separated these formal features from a ball field to the south and a meandering series of paths and shallow, shaded pools to the north. Today only the ball field and the northern strip of roadway survive, along with numerous trees and shrubs in the northern section. No parkway connection to the rest of the system was created, and the park is now separated from the Niagara River by the New York State Thruway.

The park and parkway system that Olmsted and his firm designed for Buffalo exists today partly on the ground and partly in memory and imagination. It provides the observer with a fascinating mixture of the city that is, the city that was, and the city that might have been.

Buffalo Architecture in 1940

Henry-Russell Hitchcock

In January 1940, the Albright Art Gallery mounted an exhibition commemorating 124 years of architecture in Buffalo. Henry-Russell Hitchcock, the dean of American architectural historians, organized the exhibit and wrote captions for the photographs. There was, however, no printed catalog, and for many years mimeographed copies of typescript circulated in architectural circles in Buffalo as the only written record of this impressive undertaking. When this guidebook was being prepared, the idea quite naturally suggested itself to use Professor Hitchcock's comprehensive introductory remarks to the 1940 exhibition as a preliminary chapter in the guide, for they are as relevant to the subject today as they were forty years ago. Professor Hitchcock kindly consented to this plan, and with light editing, they are printed here in their entirety.

The editors are indebted to this eminent scholar for the opportunity to publish these remarks for the first time. In recording his commentaries in this book and making them available to a wide and interested audience, we wish, on behalf of all friends of art in Buffalo, to pay a long overdue thanks to Professor Hitchcock for his authoritative tribute to the city's considerable architectural heritage.

Francis R. Kowsky

In 1893 the first edition of Baedeker's *United States* signalized with stars five Buffalo buildings: St. Paul's Episcopal Cathedral, the First Presbyterian Church, St. Louis Roman Catholic Church, Trinity Church, and the Public Library,[1] as well as Delaware Avenue, the Park and Cemetery. The two monuments for which Buffalo is best known today—the Prudential Building, by Louis Sullivan, and the Larkin Administration Building,[2] by Frank Lloyd Wright—were not mentioned, as they were not yet in existence. Most of the houses and public buildings of the first decades of Buffalo's existence were already destroyed.

The four sections of this essay deal with four stages of Buffalo's development. The first section covers the early town as it grew up between the peace which prevailed after the War of 1812 and the coming of the railroad. The second section illustrates the city of the mid-century down to the panic of 1873, which terminated the post-Civil War building boom. The last two sections deal with the latter decades of the nineteenth century and the first four of the twentieth.

Houses, churches, hotels, business buildings, elevators, and factories all serve to tell the story of Buffalo's growth, and also to display, in terms of architecture, its peculiar position as an outpost of the east and a gateway to the midwest. This is a cross section of a city, the buildings included naturally varying greatly in merit. Many will admire chiefly the early buildings, now mostly destroyed, the product of simple "builders" before architectural sophistication and eclectic taste destroyed the homogeneity of the postcolonial and Greek Revival. Others will prefer the distinguished examples of the work of eastern architects like Upjohn and Richardson and of midwesterners like Sullivan and Wright. Some will feel that the great industrial edifices, the grain elevators and newer factories, better display the spirit of Buffalo and the hope of an American architecture. The 1930s years of depression are not well represented, but the W. T. Grant Building and the Willert Park Public Housing development,[3] as well as Kleinhans Music Hall, indicate better than private construction the architectural possibilities of the mid-twentieth century.

Period I: 1816–1844

The frontier settlement at Buffalo was burned in the War of 1812. With the peace of 1815, a new town began to rise within the frame of Joseph Ellicott's plan of 1804. In 1825, the opening of the Erie Canal, of which Buffalo was the western terminus, soon brought real prosperity and a closer connection with the eastern seaboard than with the Western Reserve, to which Buffalo was the northernmost gateway. These conditions the architecture of the period illustrates. Little remains today of this first stage of Buffalo's growth. The general appearance of the community can, however, be recreated from maps, early views, and old photographs of the early houses and public buildings. These buildings differ less from those of the contemporary northeastern states than from those of the nearby rural areas of Western New York.

The Porter-Allen house,[4] in plan and mass, continues the eighteenth-century tradition. Its solid, simple form is decorated only with the small porch so frequently used on postcolonial houses everywhere. The Second Courthouse,[5] with its attenuated Ionic portico, is of a type which the rising New England cities were building in this decade. The Goodrich house[6] is very similar, though somewhat more scholarly in its use of detail. The other houses of the twenties, using the new ''row house'' formula, with door to one side of the facade and with side or rear wings, have the delicate detail and the characteristically wooden proportions of western New England houses of the same period. They were, indeed, influenced by the same source, the design manuals of Asher Benjamin. The First Church,[7] with its elaborate detail, is equally eastern in character, and a completely characteristic postcolonial meeting house.

In the 1830s a new wave of prosperity culminated in the speculative building boom of Benjamin Rathbun, which crashed in 1836. During this decade, the more solid and severe form of the Greek Revival became the basis of style; and more buildings, both commercial and residential, were built of masonry. A great simplicity of form with solid, well-cut detail, rather than any conspicuous use of Greek columns characterized this stage of development. Houses with temple porticoes were, indeed, far more rare here than in the areas just to the east and west. The castellated Gothic, moreover, made as early an appearance here as in the east, with the McKay house.

Porter-Allen house, 1816
Second Courthouse, 1816

Goodrich house, 1822
McKay house, 1837

Early Buffalo was a town laid out on a formal plan, not a city. Its houses and public buildings were designed by owners and builders, not by architects, and were built according to the rigid but gracious formula of traditional basis and classical detail. Homogeneous, and with little pretension beyond a few porticoes, the architecture of these decades, as we see it in houses and churches, in hotels and factories, was native and straightforward, if often rather dull. Never again was Buffalo architecture to be so consistent and so satisfying. We cannot return to such an idyllic stage by imitating its superficial forms. We may hope, nevertheless, that someday a similarly high and even standard of architectural quality may be regained for the vastly increased complexities of a modern industrial city.

Period II: 1844–1872

In 1843 the railroad came to Buffalo. The town at the end of the Erie Canal now became a city of increasing importance as a transportation center and the chief grain depot of America.

The first elevator in the world, the invention of Joseph Dart and Robert Dunbar, was built in Buffalo in the early 1840s. The Evans elevator,[8] one of the earliest and most famous, has, like other Buffalo buildings of the mid-century, been immortalized in the paintings of Charles Burchfield.

The new prosperity of Buffalo led to much new and pretentious building, particularly in the mid-1850s before the panic of 1857. A similar condition existed during the boom after the Civil War before the panic of 1873. At this time eastern architects first began to work in Buffalo, although the greater part of the building during these decades was still the work of carpenters and builders. The work of this period is extraordinarily interesting and of considerable variety. Although various individual buildings are perhaps of greater intrinsic architectural worth than in the previous period, the general level of design fell notoriously low. Instead of the homogeneity and anonymity of the early decades, there were now various strata and different types of building barely related to one another. Yet there is a certain consistency which links the great elevators, churches, and mansions, recognizable as mid-Victorian though difficult to describe in words.

For instance, the downtown buildings grew larger, heavier, and richer with a certain awkward use of detail characteristic of the Victorian age throughout the world. The introduction of new materials lagged. Although cast iron was used in the ground story of many buildings and for interior supports, the most important example of large-scale cast-iron construction (the German Insurance Company) typical of this period elsewhere, is very late indeed.

The building of houses in continuous rows, so typical of the vast urban expansion in the largest seaboard cities, was little exploited in Buffalo. As in the smaller cities of the northeast, however, many houses of small and even fairly large size were built in pairs. The characteristic type, both of the mansion and the cottage, was, in most American cities, the isolated one-family house. Those houses were often created by builders in groups according to standard scheme, for which the flood of new house pattern books—of which Buffalo published two[9]— provided models.

This was an age of stylistic confusion. Greek forms died slowly and the new Gothic style in house design had to vie or to coalesce with the towered Italian villa and French-roofed type derived at several removes from the splendors of Second Empire Paris.

The most characteristic Buffalo houses of the mid-nineteenth century, immortalized in the watercolors of Burchfield, are of a peculiar Victorian heaviness and clumsiness of form, with rich and turgid detail which defies stylistic analysis. Such houses are not peculiar to Buffalo and their sources may be traced in the architectural books of the 1850s and 1860s. They rise in striking contrast both to the severe and yet romantic forms of the new grain elevators and to the more archaeological work of imported eastern architects.

Buffalo, in this period, brought in Richard Upjohn, the great Gothic revivalist, and the leading American architect of the period, to build St. Paul's Episcopal Cathedral, a church which, with much justice, he considered his masterpiece. In a very different vein, the Blocher tomb, although actually much later in date, belongs in spirit to the mid-century. It is even more remarkable for its construction of enormous, beautifully hewn blocks of granite than for its fantastic sculpture.

Evans Elevator, 1847, Robert Dunbar

Buffalo Public Library, 1884, Cyrus Eidlitz
Promenade, **1927–1928, Charles Burchfield**

Period III: 1872–1900

A new and more sophisticated age opened in Buffalo when Frederick Law Olmsted was called in in 1868 to lay out parkways and parks to the north of the city in the area toward which the residential district was rapidly expanding. These parkways, with their repeated rows of great trees, are the finest in America, and form the setting of as handsome and varied a group of late nineteenth- and early twentieth-century houses as are to be found in this country.

With Olmsted came H. H. Richardson, destined to be the great leader of American architecture from the 1870s to the 1890s. In the Dorsheimer house he was only feeling his way, on the basis of his French training and superior sense of proportion, out of the Victorian morass. In the Buffalo State Hospital, his earliest important commission and one of his largest, he really found, in the years between 1870 and 1872, his personal style. This style was much imitated here and elsewhere in the next score of years. It is interesting to follow the stages of his self-discovery, from the splendidly articulated plan through the awkward first facade project with its ugly detail to the final superb romantic mass of the central pavilion. The bold silhouette, the balanced proportions, and the individual fusion of the Romanesque and late Gothic detail are already almost completely mature.

Richardson's project for Trinity Church was never executed, which is perhaps as well, since the exterior was overpicturesque. The Byzantine spaces of its interior, however, are echoed in more suave and historical form in Green and Wicks's First Presbyterian Church. Its exterior is an excellent, if somewhat rambling, composition wholly unrelated to the interior, done in the supposedly "Revived Romanesque" style derived from Richardson's mature work.

Another derivation is the Coatsworth-Pardee-Wright house in Soldiers Place,[10] which owes its wholly remarkable quality to the fact that the Buffalo architect William Lansing made what is practically a line-for-line copy of Richardson's finest wooden house, the Stoughton house in Cambridge.

In the 1890s Richardson's pupils, McKim, Mead and White, leaders of the reaction against his picturesque, medieval style, built several houses in Buffalo. Possibly the implications of the academic reaction, with its return to formal symmetry and archaeological correctness of detail, are more effectively presented in the work of George Cary and in many characteristic houses of the nineties and the first quarter of this century.

Employing Upjohn, Richardson, Eidlitz, and McKim, Mead and White, and with its own architects educated in the east, Buffalo might seem to have become architecturally, in the late nineteenth century, an eastern city. It turned its back on the elevators, those great industrial monuments which continued to speak of its close connection with the midwest and displayed the possibilities of building for new purposes and on a new scale. Yet, as a matter of fact, the two best known buildings in Buffalo of this period are by Chicago architects and serve to make plain that Buffalo was even more, around 1900, the gateway to the midwest than it had been earlier.

The Guaranty Building, now the Prudential, is not Sullivan's first skyscraper, but many find it his best. Completed in 1896, it makes use of the new skeleton construction developed in Chicago a decade previous. It was soon to revolutionize American building methods. A second skyscraper, built in Buffalo the same year by another famous Chicago architect, was the Ellicott Square Building, by D. H. Burnham. While Burnham attempted, like the eastern architects of the day, to clothe the new construction and the new scale of his monster building in the academic Renaissance vocabulary of masonry introduced by McKim, Mead and White, Sullivan continued with his Guaranty Building the development of a free and expressive clothing of a metal frame. He had first tried this successfully six years earlier with the Wainwright Building in St. Louis.

The grace and elegance of his design, the vertical expression so appropriate to a building rising isolated like a tower above its neighbors, are not lost in the web of rich ornamentation which Sullivan used on his terra-cotta surfaces. Sullivan was not concerned with major problems of design alone; indeed, he was more interested in the new grammar of ornament. Some of the ornamental work on this building, particularly the ironwork of the elevator cage, represents perhaps the last really great work in decorative design created in the western world.

Period IV: 1900–1940

At the turn of the century downtown Buffalo was predominantly midwestern in character, with its great elevators and Chicago skyscrapers. Uptown Buffalo, with its mansions and churches, was almost wholly eastern in character. Its secondary streets, however, lined a few feet apart with isolated houses, whose crude details echo the styles of the great mansions, are perhaps more typical of the midwest. In the early years of this century, curiously enough, the balance was almost to be reversed. Buffalo's continued contributions to architecture were to remain primarily midwestern until the World War.

The Larkin Administration Building (designed in 1903–1904 and destroyed in 1950), by Frank Lloyd Wright, is doubtless better known throughout the world than Sullivan's Guaranty Building. Although not a factory, it was nonetheless almost the first attempt to find a truly architectural expression for industrial building. It was extravagantly admired and frequently imitated throughout Europe, where it played its part in that development of modern industrial architecture to which all contemporary building owes so much. In these decades, however, Wright was at his best in domestic architecture. Today the four houses he built for clients associated with the Larkin Company will perhaps strike us as finer than the Larkin Building. The house on Tillinghast Place in particular may well be compared with the finest houses Wright built during the same period in Chicago suburbs.

The appearance of Wright in Buffalo had little effect, beyond these five buildings of his, upon the general character of the local architecture. Only in the Larkin Warehouse, by a Boston firm, curiously enough, and possibly in George Cary's Pierce-Arrow offices, is there any continuation of the line of Wright's industrial architecture.

The General Electric Tower by Esenwein and Johnson, with its Renaissance effervescent termination above a utilitarian shaft, is more typical of the commercial building of the period before 1929. The superficially modernized forms of the City Hall and the New York Central station are not essentially different in spirit.

Residential architecture in Buffalo to 1940 has continued the tradition of suave imitation of past styles established by eastern architects in the nineties.

Elevator cage, Prudential Building, 1895–1896, Adler and Sullivan

W. T. Grant Building, 1939, Alfred S. Alschuler and Raymond Loewy

In comparison with the later skyscrapers and houses, which might have been built anywhere in America during the first third of this century, the grain elevators and industrial machinery of Buffalo stand out for their originality, their splendid scale, and clean design. Such a comparison is not altogether fair, yet it does appear that Buffalo's factories, the Grant Building,[11] and its housing developments are more closely related to the American tradition of engineering architecture than to the more sophisticated and subtle modernism of Sullivan and Wright.

Buffalo may well be proud of the architectural story outlined here and hope for an architectural future as brilliant as, and perhaps more homogeneous than, the period 1840 to 1940. Two plans, the early one of Ellicott and the park developments of Olmsted, neither one adequately continued, indicate frames within which Buffalo for a time sought to discipline its growth. The hope of the future must lie at least as much in the establishment of a new and broader frame of planning, as in the erection of single buildings of distinction. The future ought also to provide some means of preserving the finer moments of the past, instead of allowing that indiscriminate destruction which has, during the present century, removed far more excellent buildings than have been built.

Notes

1 Demolished in 1960, it stood on Lafayette Square at the site of the present Buffalo and Erie County Public Library.

2 Demolished in 1950. See the "Lost Buffalo" section.

3 Now Alfred D. Price Housing.

4 Demolished in 1911, it stood on the corner of Niagara and Ferry streets.

5 It stood on Lafayette Square, where the present Buffalo and Erie County Public Library stands. It was demonlished in 1876.

6 It was also known as the Hoyt House after it was moved to Amherst Street opposite Nottingham. It was demolished in 1946.

7 It was located on Shelton Square, near where the present Main Place Mall–Erie Savings Bank Building stands.

8 Demolished in 1939.

9 Oliver P. Smith, *The Domestic Architect: Comprising a Series of Original Designs for Rural and Ornamental Cottages* (Buffalo: Phinney & Co., 1854) and Charles P. Dwyer, *The Economic Cottage Builder; or Cottages for Men of Small Means* (Buffalo: Wanzer, McKim & Co., 1856).

10 Moved to Lincoln Woods Lane.

11 Demolished in 1981.

Niagara River
Lake Erie

The City of Buffalo

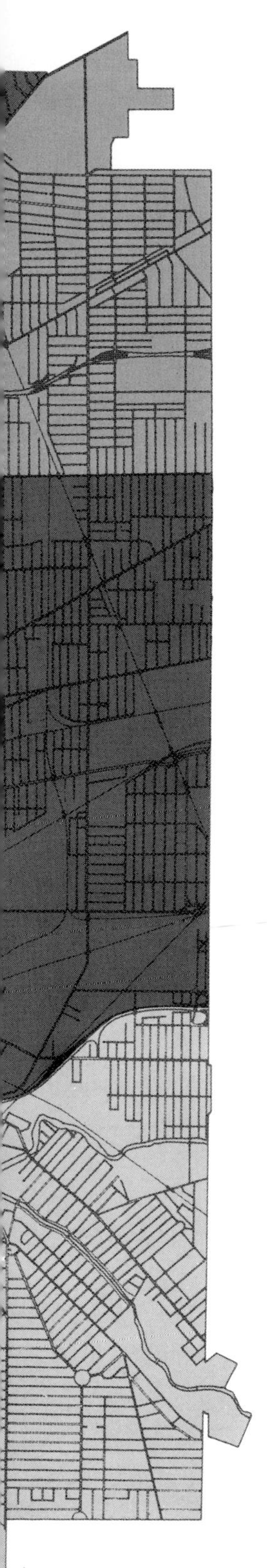

1 Downtown

As pioneer settlers always have, the first residents of Buffalo settled near the waterways. Well before the completion of the Erie Canal in 1825, the Buffalo Creek had been the focal point of whatever life the settlers in the area—the Seneca Indians, the trappers, and the surveyors—had made. In fact, Black Rock, an independent village to the north with a natural sheltered harbor, would have been a more logical western terminus for the canal than Buffalo, whose waterfront was laid bare to the buffeting of Lake Erie's winds and waves. However, under the leadership of Samuel D. Wilkeson, Buffalo's harbor was dredged and a breakwall constructed, which resulted in the location of the terminal point of the Erie Canal at the mouth of the Buffalo Creek. Thus, the area around lower Main Street was solidified as Buffalo's center. The dominance of this area increased during the 1840s and 1850s as Buffalo, located near the eastern end of the Great Lakes, became one of the most important inland ports in the country.

Main Street looking south from Virginia Street

While the population grew rapidly, the settled area remained relatively unchanged as the absence of adequate public transportation forced people to compete for space within the dense and overbuilt areas of town hemmed in between Division Street, the Buffalo Creek, Michigan Avenue, and the Niagara River. Within this compact area were located docks and piers, grain elevators, ship factories, breweries, tanneries, lumber and livestock yards, and iron foundries. Here also, somehow mixed into this cauldron of urban growth, were the homes, schools, churches, and markets of the many people, primarily Irish immigrants, who in the middle of the nineteenth century called this section of Buffalo home. The railroads, given huge areas of street-level rights-of-way by a city government eager for economic growth, provided yet another level of intense land use. With terminals at Exchange Street and on the waterfront, the railroads attracted still more jobs, people, and industry to lower Main Street and the near East Side of Buffalo.

Contributing to these economic, demographic, and transportation developments was the hand of the city planner, which had already begun to have an impact on the physical form of the city. Commissioned by the Holland Land Company in 1797 to survey its massive holdings in Western New York, Joseph Ellicott, influenced by his brother's work as Pierre L'Enfant's associate in Washington, D.C., brought to Buffalo, then called New Amsterdam, the ideas of baroque city planning. Applying the lessons that L'Enfant himself had learned at Versailles, Ellicott in 1804 created a radial street system centered on Niagara Square that belied the settlement's status as hardly more than a frontier outpost with fewer than 100 inhabitants. Ellicott's plan was an accurate reflection of the hopes and aspirations that the original founders had for the city.

Many land-use decisions in the first half of the nineteenth century were made not by surveyors and planners, but by real estate developers. None was more active on the local scene than Benjamin Rathbun, a businessman-entrepreneur typical of the urban frontier. By the middle of the 1830s Rathbun had built the city's most popular hotel and established the first horse-drawn omnibus line on Main Street. Although Rathbun's fortunes collapsed in the nationwide Panic of 1837, his building activities had already remade Main Street. Rathbun built fifty-one brick stores ranging in height from three to five stories, a warehouse, the Eagle Street Theater, and thirty-one dwellings valued at $4000 to $15,000.

It was not until the post–Civil War era that Buffalo developed a specialized central business district, or downtown, as we know it today. Many forces, including a rapidly expanding and increasingly complex economy, contributed to this development. The city's population grew from 155,000 in 1880 to 256,000 in 1890. This growth, combined with the introduction of the electric streetcar system in the late 1880s, enabled downtown to emerge as the focal point of a metropolitan region, by encouraging residential decentralization while allowing people from all over the city to travel downtown for the price of a nickel. Thousands did, and the changes in land use which followed were unprecedented.

One result was that the office tower replaced the church steeple as the symbol of downtown by the early twentieth century. The Dun Building (1894–1895) and the D. S. Morgan Building (1895–1896) towered over their mid-nineteenth-century neighbors on Pearl Street. Nearby, the Shelton Square area became the center for business headquarters as the Erie County Savings Bank (1890–1893), the Prudential (Guaranty) Building (1895–1896), and the Ellicott Square Building (1895–1896) were constructed. In the process, the remnants of an earlier era, including homes, churches, and small office blocks, were demolished. Structural steel and elevators were among the major advances in building technology which made the large-scale structures possible. Escalating real estate values in the downtown area also encouraged more intensive land use.

Also built during this period were grand hotels, which catered to the growing number of transient businessmen: the Iroquois (1890) at Washington and Eagle, the Lafayette (1904) on Lafayette Square, the original Statler (1906) at Washington and South Division, and the Hotel Buffalo (1908) at Washington and Swan. Retail business boomed as well. Some stores, such as Hengerer's, Flint and Kent's, and J. N. Adam's, expanded their Main Street facilities, while others, such as Hens and Kelly's, built new stores. Denton, Cottier and Daniels opened their music emporium on Court Street in 1906.

As downtown became increasingly commercialized, it lost its appeal as a residential section for all but the city's poorest residents. As the number of people moving out of downtown increased, old downtown churches were either demolished or converted to uses more suitable to a modern central business district. With many of its congregation now living in what had been outlying areas earlier in the century, the trustees of the First Presbyterian Church, located since 1821 at Shelton Square, decided to move to a "neighborhood not so shut in by business." Following the sale of the church property to Erie County Savings Bank, the congregation moved to Symphony Circle in 1889. Churches also gave way to large, garish theaters, as downtown became the entertainment center of the metropolis. In 1904 the North Presbyterian Church on Main near Huron was demolished and replaced by the Hippodrome Theater. Eight years later the Central Presbyterian Church at Pearl

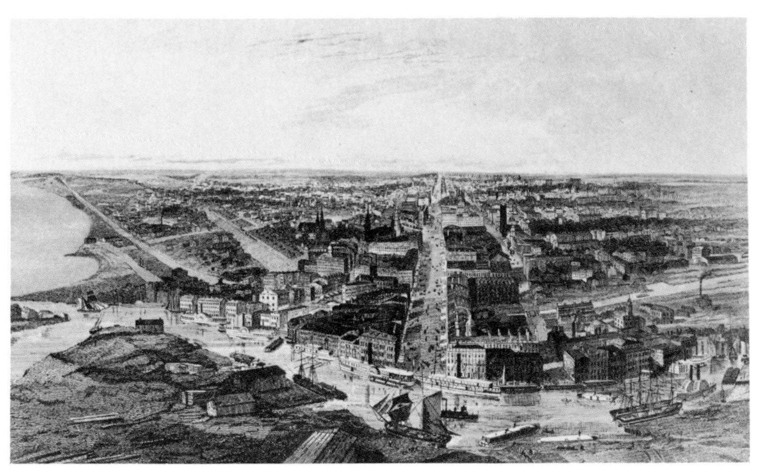

Lower Main Street, circa 1855
Lafayette Square, circa 1905

and Genesee gave way to the Majestic Theater. And in 1906 the Gothic-style St. John's Episcopal Church, built in 1846, was demolished for the construction of the Statler Hotel across from the hive of offices in the Ellicott Square Building.

Not only the skyline but the streetscape, too, was changing dramatically. As Lafayette Square became an important link in the growing commercial network of downtown, its days as the last park in the heart of the city were numbered. In 1912 the Common Council voted to extend Broadway through Lafayette Square to Main Street, and "to devote to street purposes all that part of the Square except a small circle around the Soldiers and Sailors Monument."

Even residential areas on the periphery of the central business district were not immune to the expansion of downtown. Since the 1850s the beautiful, tree-lined mall of Johnson Park had been a venerable and exclusive area, within walking distance of downtown yet far enough away that its residential quality was preserved. However, because its location on an east-west axis blocked vehicular access to downtown, in 1907 the Common Council approved the extension of Elmwood Avenue through Johnson Park. That extension and the building of a streetcar line signaled the beginning of Johnson Park's decline as an elegant, inner-city residential neighborhood, a trend reversed only since the mid-1960s.

The exodus of affluent residents paralleled the arrival of thousands of Italian immigrants in the early years of the twentieth century, who were attracted to the waterfront because of the plentiful jobs available. Hemmed in between the Niagara River and Niagara Square, their church, St. Anthony of Padua, still stands, although the original inhabitants of the area have been displaced by urban renewal projects.

By World War I, the character of downtown had been radically altered from what it had been even twenty-five years previously, in terms of scale, function, and image. The building boom of the 1920s, which followed the hiatus caused by World War I, contributed many new structures but did not affect the basic pattern of development which had been established in the prewar years. The Niagara Mohawk Building (1912) at Washington and Genesee, the Liberty National

Erie Street Mall
Downtown skyline from the Erie Basin Marina

Bank (1925) at Main and Court, and the Rand Building (1929) on Lafayette Square surpassed in height their late nineteenth-century predecessors, if they did not equal their architectural accomplishment. It should be noted that the construction of City Hall (1929–1931), which closed off Court Street on the west side of Niagara Square, represented the first major departure from Joseph Ellicott's 1804 plan.

The Great Depression and World War II constrained building activity in the downtown area, as had World War I. Then the city's population began to decline, from 580,000 in 1950 to under 350,000 by 1980. On highways built with state and federal aid, thousands of longtime city residents flocked to newly built suburban homes, many of which were insured by the federal government. Virtually every major local planning decision of the postwar period also undermined Buffalo's future, from the construction of the new stadium in Orchard Park to the location of the new State University campus in suburban Amherst. Downtown and the central city neighborhoods began to decline precipitously under the impact of massive private and public disinvestment.

Since the 1960s, policy makers have tried a variety of renewal strategies to stem the decline. Main Place Mall, M&T Bank, and Marine Midland Center all represent part of the early effort to improve the tax base and image of downtown. Most recently, the city has undertaken several additional projects: a seventy-acre residential and commercial waterfront complex; the entertainment district renewal and the nearby hotel and office developments at Main Street and Genesee Street; the light rail rapid transit system on Main Street; and a new center for Erie Community College to be located in the Old Post Office on Ellicott Street. Light industrial development is also beginning to occur on the east side of downtown, along the newly constructed Elm-Oak arterial.

It is true that Buffalo's economic base has been eroded by major changes in the national and international economy, and that the long-range success of downtown and neighborhood revitalization remains to be seen. However, an enormous bank of strength, commitment, and pride still exists in Buffalo, and while the battle to survive promises to be difficult and long, the will to win is great.

Downtown

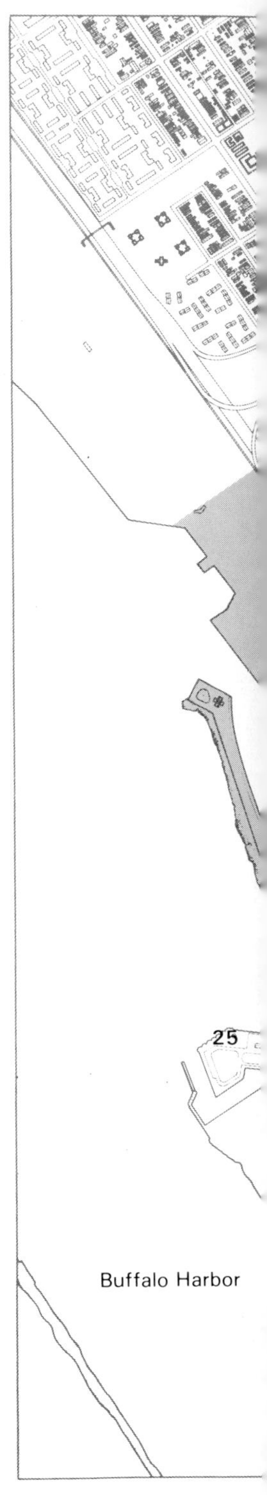

1 McKinley Monument

2 City Hall

3 City Court Building

4 Buffalo Athletic Club

5 U.S. Post Office

6 Buffalo State Office Building

7 Statler Hotel

8 Convention Center

9 St. Anthony of Padua Church

10 Shoreline Apartments

11 Waterfront Community Center

12 Illuminating Gas Company

13 WKBW-TV Studios

14 Buffalo Hilton Hotel

15 Title Guarantee Company

16 Old County Hall

17 Rath County Office Building

Delaware Avenue
Franklin Street
Main Street
Oak Street
Elm Street
West Tupper Street
Elmwood Avenue
Niagara Street
Genesee Street
Michigan Avenue
Broadway
Court Street
Church Street
South Division Street
Erie Street
Seneca Street
New York State Thruway
Buffalo River
1
2
3
4
5
6
7
8
9
10
11
12
13
14
15
16
17
18
19
20
21
22
23
24
27
28
29
30
31
32
33
34
35
36
37
38
39
40
41
42
43
44
45
46
47
48
49
50
51
52
53
54
55
56
57

18 76 Church Street

19 Prudential (Guaranty) Building

20 St. Paul's Episcopal Cathedral

21 Dun Building

22 St. Joseph's Cathedral

23 Merit Building

24 76–92 Pearl Street

25 Buffalo Lighthouse

26 Erie Basin Marina

27 Marine Drive Apartments

28 Buffalo Naval and Servicemen's Park and Museum

29 Memorial Auditorium

30 Buffalo News Building

31 Marine Midland Center

32 Dennis Building

33 Ellicott Square Building

34 Old Post Office

35 Fitch House

36 Alling and Cory

37 Metropolitan Transportation Center

38 M&T Bank Building

39 Main Place Mall–Erie Savings Bank Building

40 Liberty Bank Building

41 Lafayette Square

42 Brisbane Building

43 Lafayette Hotel

44 Buffalo and Erie County Public Library

45 Rand Building

46 10 Lafayette Square Building

47 Buffalo Savings Bank Building

48 Niagara Mohawk Building

49 Market Arcade

50 St. Michael's Church

51 Shea's Buffalo Center for the Performing Arts

52 Calumet Building

53 Federal Office Building

54 Graystone Hotel

55 WGR-TV Studios

56 Asbury United Methodist Church

57 Vars Building

1 McKinley Monument, 1907
Niagara Square
Architects: Carrère and Hastings
Conceptual plan: D. H. Burnham
Sculptor: A. Philmister Proctor

Niagara Square was laid out by Joseph Ellicott to function as the hub of the city, somewhat in the manner of Capitol Hill in Washington, D.C., the plan of which Ellicott knew well from having assisted his brother Andrew in surveying L'Enfant's city. The twentieth century, however, has not been sympathetic to Ellicott's concept, and many of the streets radiating from the square have been blocked by nearby buildings. City Hall blocks the extension of Court Street west of Niagara Square; Main Place Mall stands astride Niagara Street; the Convention Center terminates the vista to the northeast along Genesee Street; and the Charles R. Turner Parking Ramp is built over West Genesee Street.

For many years Niagara Square itself was a poorly defined space. In 1874 Olmsted presented a plan for it that created a series of planted angles between incoming streets and envisioned a Civil War memorial arch (never erected) after a design by H. H. Richardson to stand where Delaware Avenue enters the square from the north. In the center of the square, for which Olmsted had proposed a large basin, stands the city's memorial to President William McKinley, who was assassinated while attending the Pan-American Exposition. D. H. Burnham, who was called in to consult on the project, suggested the appropriateness of an obelisk with fountains at the base and decided where it should be placed. Carrère and Hastings, the actual designers of the monument, were the architects in charge of the Exposition and had also worked with Burnham at the 1893 Chicago fair, where similar obelisks had been erected. A. Philmister Proctor, a well-known animal sculptor who had executed several pieces for the Pan-American Exposition, carved the sleeping lions, symbols of strength, and the turtles, emblematic of eternal life.

Looking from City Hall around the square, one sees unexceptional but well-mannered buildings, except for the City Court, with its brutalist design. City Hall, planned by a man trained in the Beaux-Arts tradition, capitalizes on the advantages of the site and dramatically terminates the axis along Court Street from Lafayette Square.

2 **Buffalo City Hall, 1929–1931**
65 Niagara Square
Architects: George J. Dietel and John J. Wade (chief designer), with Sullivan W. Jones

Portico frieze: Albert T. Stewart, New York City
Lobby murals: William de Leftwich Dodge, New York City
Detail sculpture: René Chambellan, New York City
Timbrel tile ceiling vault: Rafael Guastavino Company
Observatory on 28th floor, 3-story walkup from 25th floor
(Interior photo shows the Common Council Chamber.)

In the words of its architect, John J. Wade, City Hall ''expresses primarily the masculinity, power, and purposeful energy of an industrial community.'' Wade, who studied architecture at the Beaux-Arts Institute in New York, admired greatly the romantically futuristic visions of skyscraper cities drawn by Hugh Ferriss. In City Hall's soaring mass and dramatic nighttime lighting he embodied essential elements of Ferriss's architectural fantasies.

One of the outstanding Art Deco public buildings in the country, City Hall is appropriately decorated. Above the eight giant columns of the main entrance, a carved frieze of twenty-one figures represents aspects of the city's cultural and economic life. The bronze doors of the entrance bear symbols of the Indian tribes who once inhabited the region. At the corners of the building stand bronze statues by Bryant Baker of Millard Fillmore and Grover Cleveland, the two U.S. Presidents who came from Buffalo. And high above the square the brightly colored roof of the central tower glitters day and night, a festive crown for the Queen City of the Lakes.

The observatory on the twenty-eighth floor affords spectacular views of Lake Erie and the city from about 330 feet up. From here one can best appreciate how Ellicott's radial street plan centers upon Niagara Square.

On the inside, City Hall has many richly ornamented spaces. Decorations include marble floors, mosaic ceilings, sculpted piers, and colorful murals. Most ornate are the entrance lobby and the surrounding corridors and the Common Council chamber with its superb sunburst skylight window.

The Architectural Museum and Resource Center is located on the twenty-fifth and twenty-eighth floors, until the completion of the Prudential Building restoration.

3 **City Court Building, 1971–1974**
50 Delaware Avenue, Niagara Square
Architects: Pfohl, Roberts and Biggie
Plaza sculpture: Kenneth Snelson

The windowless walls, which present an impenetrable facade to Niagara Square, were designed to protect the courtrooms and judges' chambers from outside distractions, as well as to accommodate sculpture and define space.

4 **Buffalo Athletic Club, 1921–1924**
Niagara Square at Delaware Avenue
Architects: Edward B. Green and Son

5 **U.S. Post Office, 1935–1936**
(formerly Federal Courthouse)
64 Court Street, Niagara Square
Architects: Bley and Lyman, with Edward B. Green and Son

6 **Buffalo State Office Building, 1928–1931**
65 Court Street, Niagara Square
Architects: Edward B. Green and Son with Albert Hart Hopkins

7 **Statler Hotel, 1921–1923**
107 Delaware Avenue, Niagara Square
Architects: George B. Post and Sons

8 **Buffalo Convention Center, 1976–1978**
Franklin Street at Genesee Street
Architects: Di Donato Renaldo Associates

9 **St. Anthony of Padua Roman Catholic Church, 1891**
160 Court Street
Architect: Michael Sheehan
Addition: 1904–1906, Cesari Antozzi

10 Shoreline Apartments, 1971–1974
Niagara Street and Seventh Street, at Mohawk Street
Architect: Paul Rudolph

The stepped profile of the low-rise buildings, with their garden courts, balconies, and simple shed roofs, demonstrates the unmistakable style of one of the first American architects to experiment with alternatives to high-rise apartment towers in favor of a more human scale.

11 **Waterfront School and Community Center, 1974–1977**
95 Fourth Street
Architects: Hess and Gorey, based on Paul Rudolph's concept

12 **Illuminating Gas Company, 1848**
249 West Genesee Street
Additions: 1859, John H. Selkirk, existing facade; 1877, coal storage and boiler plant
National Register of Historic Places

The site of the gas works, once on the shores of both Lake Erie and the Erie Canal, facilitated the delivery of coal for the manufacture of illuminating gas. The 250-foot facade of brick, dressed with ashlar masonry, is the building's most outstanding architectural feature.

13 **WKBW-TV Studios, 1979**
7 Broadcast Plaza
Architects: Stieglitz, Stieglitz, Tries

Harbinger of the "suburbanization" of downtown with its plantings, lawns, and parking lots, Channel 7's brushed stainless steel exterior is part of an elaborately contrived "energy-responsible" environmental system that uses 120,000 gallons of water as a thermal flywheel.

14 **Buffalo Hilton Hotel at the Waterfront, 1979–1980**
Church Street at Lower Terrace
Architect: Clement Chen and Associates

15 Title Guarantee Company, 1833
110 Franklin Street
Builder: Benjamin Rathbun
Conversion: 1880, F. W. Caulkins

The oldest building in downtown Buffalo, the Title Guarantee Company was originally constructed as the First Unitarian Church. Stephen G. Austin bought the building in 1880. He engaged F. W. Caulkins to convert the structure into offices. Caulkins raised it one story and added several bays on the Eagle Street side, but retained the dignified facade on Franklin Street. With its giant pilasters and almost Albertian sense of proportion and planarity it is more in the spirit of earlier romantic classicism than of the contemporary Greek Revival. For a number of years, Green and Wicks, Buffalo's most prolific architectural firm, had its office here.

16 Old County Hall, 1871–1876 (formerly City and County Hall)
92 Franklin Street
Architect: Andrew J. Warner
Sculpture: Giovanni F. Sala, central tower figures
Renovation: 1925, Harold Jewett Cook; 1963–1980, Milstein, Wittek and Davis
National Register of Historic Places

County Hall, where Grover Cleveland began his political career, is the only important example in Buffalo of High Victorian Gothic, the preeminent style of the Gilded Age. Symmetrical and monochromatic, the building, which was designed by the Rochester architect Andrew Jackson Warner, is a particular conservative version of that baroque phase of Gothic Revival. Perhaps Warner's experience as supervising architect of Richardson's Buffalo State Hospital had influenced him toward more severe and monumental expression. The boldest feature of his design is the bulky central tower bearing colossal figures of Justice, Mechanical Arts, Agriculture, and Commerce.

On the inside, only the registry of deed room, with its tall, cast-iron columns decorated with incised ornament, survives unchanged from Warner's time. The rest of the interior was thoroughly remodeled in 1925 by Harold Jewett Cook, a local architect well known for his many bank designs, into a rather typical example of "bureaucratic classical."

County Hall occupies the site of Franklin Square, the city's first cemetery. It was here on December 10, 1813, that Colonel Cyrenius Chapin surrendered the village to the British, who, contrary to their assurances, proceeded to burn the town. In the 1870s, Olmsted proposed that the grounds around the new building be landscaped to create a visual base for the structure in the manner of his nearly contemporary plans for the Capitol at Washington.

17 **Edward A. Rath County Office Building, 1969–1971**
95 Franklin Street
Architects: Milstein, Wittek and Davis with Backus, Crane and Love
Lobby Mural: Walter A. Prochownik

18 **76 Church Street, circa 1870**

Now used for professional offices, this is the oldest extant residential structure in the heart of Buffalo's central business district.

19 **Prudential Building, 1895–1896**
(formerly Guaranty Building)
28 Church Street
Architects: Adler and Sullivan
National Historic Landmark
(Detail photos show terra-cotta decoration on window archway; original hallway interior; stairway.)

The Prudential Building was intended to be named after Hascal L. Taylor (1830–1894), the Buffalonian who commissioned Dankmar Adler (1844–1900) and Louis Sullivan (1856–1924) to build what he wanted to be "the largest and best office building in the city." Unfortunately, he died in November of 1894 just before construction plans were to be publicly announced.

The Guaranty Construction Company of Chicago, which was to construct the building for Taylor, bought the property and completed the project. Construction began in 1895, and the Guaranty Building was occupied on March 1,

PRUDENTIAL

1896. It was renamed the Prudential Building about two years after it was completed at the time of refinancing through the Prudential Insurance Company.

Louis Sullivan called the Prudential Building a ''sister'' to his prototype skyscraper, the Wainwright Building (1890–1892) in St. Louis, both designed within the decade following William Le Baron Jenney's Home Insurance Building (1884) in Chicago, the first tall, metallic-framed structure. With the Wainwright, Sullivan first expressed the essential nature of the new tall buildings—the power of their verticality.

The Prudential, his most mature skyscraper, is a glorious refinement of the Wainwright. Its ruddy terra-cotta facade is embellished with Sullivan's rich foliate and geometric ornament, some of which was detailed by George Grant Elmslie, Adler and Sullivan's chief draftsman. The original projecting glass storefronts and decorative iron grilles enclosing the elevators have been removed. The lobbies' open spatial character and the stairwells havc been compromised by various alterations, but much remains of the original interior riches—the marble mosaics, the exquisite stained-glass lobby skylight, and the intricately designed iron stairway balusters.

Sullivan had a deep commitment to democratic ideals, natural forms, and to evolving a truly American architecture free of neoclassical excesses. The Prudential expresses his ideas in its integration of bold, uplifting vertical lines, intricate ornament, and materials.

Sullivan sought to enrich the city's workplace, and the Prudential still attests to his success in doing so. After a widespread community preservation campaign over the last five years, it is planned to restore the masterwork as faithfully as possible to its original character as a high-quality office building.

The Architectural Museum and Resource Center, located in the City Hall Observatory, features displays of Sullivan's ornamental artifacts among other materials about American architecture. The museum will return to the Prudential Building upon completion of restoration.

20 **St. Paul's Episcopal Cathedral, 1849–1851**
Church Street at Pearl Street
Architect: Richard Upjohn
Tower: 1870–1871
Interior and roof rebuilt: 1888, Robert W. Gibson with Cyrus K. Porter
National Register of Historic Places

Upjohn's Trinity Church of 1840–1846 in New York City brought to America the influence of the theories of the pioneer Gothic revivalist, A. W. N. Pugin, who loved the great cathedrals of the Age of Faith. St. Paul's, which Upjohn is said to have regarded even more highly than Trinity, derives instead from the later notions of the Anglican ecclesiologists who found the requirements of church building best fulfilled in medieval parish churches. Here the architect sought inspiration in the rural churches of thirteenth-century Britain, the style known as Early English, which is distinguished by lancet windows and simple moldings. Capitalizing on the freedom that this medieval precedent allowed, Upjohn created a building asymmetrical in plan and elevation that picturesquely embraces its irregular site.

The interior of St. Paul's, including the handsome hammerbeam roof, was rebuilt by Robert W. Gibson after an 1888 fire that gutted the church. Gibson revised Upjohn's original scheme by adding a clerestory, transept arches, and detailing from the Decorated style of the fourteenth century. The naturalistically carved foliage capitals and curvilinear tracery of the chancel window are characteristics of this more ornate phase of English Gothic. The whitewashed walls of the interior are true to neither Upjohn's nor Gibson's scheme, for both of them employed colored decoration. The exterior of the church, which was one of the first buildings in Buffalo to use Medina sandstone, remains basically as Upjohn conceived it.

21 **Dun Building, 1894–1895**
110 Pearl Street at Erie Street Mall
Architects: Green and Wicks

The Dun Building, clad in yellow Roman brick, represents an attempt to apply the principles of neoclassicism, an inherently horizontal style of architecture, to the design of the new tall office building. With questionable results, Green and Wicks emulated the example of George B. Post's New York Produce Exchange (1882) and used giant arches to organize the elevations. The aesthetic problem was matched by a serious structural one. The building's narrow width demanded that special attention be paid to wind bracing. This was achieved by supporting the internal steel frame with exterior load-bearing masonry walls.

22 St. Joseph's Cathedral, 1851–1855

50 Franklin Street
Architect: Patrick C. Keeley
Tower: 1862
Parish House: 1875
Renovated: 1976–1977, Trautman Associates

In contrast to Upjohn's highly picturesque and historically accurate Gothic design for St. Paul's, Keeley's design for St. Joseph's represents the more symmetrical and generalized Gothic common to mid-nineteenth-century Catholic churches. Although A. W. N. Pugin, the father of the ecclesiastical Gothic Revival and the reputed teacher of Keeley, was a Catholic convert, the Roman church never fully embraced the British Gothic Revival. More concerned with accommodating large congregations than with expressing the true principles of ecclesiology, Catholic churches like St. Joseph's had deeper affinities with Continental cathedrals than with English rural parish churches. Especially French in the design of St. Joseph's is the facade, with its twin towers (the north spire was never built), rose window, and triple portals.

Keeley, an Irish immigrant architect whose office was in Brooklyn, enjoyed a flourishing practice as a designer of Catholic churches. A number of early cathedrals in eastern cities were built from his plans, including the immense Cathedral of the Holy Cross in Boston (1865), for which St. Joseph's seems to have been the prototype.

23 Merit Building, 1915

35 Franklin Street
Engineers: Lockwood, Greene & Company

This is a factory-warehouse building, originally the Walker Shoe Company, in an unusual high-rise format. The site was originally on the frontier between the downtown business district and dockside manufacturers.

24 76–92 Pearl Street, circa 1870–1890

This group of buildings, which once housed cabinetry and furniture manufacturers, is typical of the nineteenth-century cast-iron and brick commercial structures that once stood in the city.

25 Buffalo Lighthouse, 1833
U.S. Coast Guard Base at the Buffalo Harbor
Restored: 1961

Built in 1833, the Buffalo Lighthouse is one of the oldest such structures on the Great Lakes. It replaced the first Buffalo Lighthouse of 1818, which stood closer to shore. Made of ashlar limestone and bluestone, and occupying a vantage point at the end of a man-made stone breakwater, it rises 44 feet above the harbor. To nineteenth-century Great Lakes mariners it was known as "Chinaman's Light" because of the fancied Chinese-hat shape of the top, the first landmark visible to an arriving lake vessel.

Forming a part of the seal of the city, the lighthouse is sometimes regarded as a symbol of Buffalo. Threatened by demolition in the late 1950s, the lighthouse was saved in 1961, without federal or state aid of any kind, by the action of community-minded people and the Buffalo and Erie County Historical Society. The project marks the beginning of the preservation movement in the city.

26 **Erie Basin Marina, 1970–1973**
Architects: Di Donato Renaldo Associates

The Buffalo skyline can be appreciated from the vantage point of the marina's observation tower.

27 **Marine Drive Apartments, 1950–1952**
(originally Dante Place Housing)
205 Marine Drive at the waterfront
Architects: Backus, Crane and Love

Built as public housing, the Marine Drive apartments are now privately operated. The high-rise towers were not successful as low-income family housing, but have proven attractive to other segments of the population, including downtown workers.

28 Buffalo Naval and Servicemen's Park and Museum, 1979
1 Naval Park Cove, behind Memorial Auditorium on the Buffalo River
Architects: Stieglitz, Stieglitz, Tries

A visitor orientation and exhibition center for the retired naval ships, tanks, and other venerable war machines that have come to rest on water and land under the Skyway, the building is designed in an iron-clad idiom that would be almost too sympathetic to its subject matter were it not for its rousing red paint job.

29 Memorial Auditorium, 1938–1940
140 Main Street
Architects: Green and James
Renovation: 1967, Pfohl, Roberts and Biggie

30 Buffalo News Office Building, 1971–1973
Washington Street at Scott Street
Architect: Edward Durrell Stone

A skylit two-story atrium forms the core of the administrative offices on the fourth and fifth floors. The architect, an early proponent of the International Style, in later years turned to neoclassical forms as a source of enrichment for his work.

31 Marine Midland Center, 1969–1974
Main Street at Seneca Street
Architects: Skidmore, Owings and Merrill (San Francisco Office)
Plaza sculpture: Ronald Bladen

Recalling the position of the Pan-Am Building above Park Avenue in New York, the Marine Midland Center terminates the long vista down Main Street. Isolated from the surrounding streets by an elevated plaza from which the austere tower (Buffalo's tallest building) rises, the building emphatically marks the end of the downtown commercial district.

32 Dennis Building, circa 1873
251–257 Main Street

Cast iron, the revolutionary nineteenth-century building material, was produced in quantity in Buffalo, which is strategically located between the ore fields of the upper Great Lakes and the coal mines of Pennsylvania. Several important architectural ironwork firms existed here after 1850, including the Eagle Iron Works, Washington Iron Works, and Tifft Iron Works. These names can still be found on many buildings in the city. The Dennis Building is the only surviving local example of a facade entirely of iron. Unfortunately, modernization of the ground floor has obscured any identifying plaques and it is not known if the building was the product of a local manufacturer. More common to Buffalo than the multistoried iron front are facades consisting of ground-floor iron columns supporting upper stories of brick in which decorative features, such as window sills and caps, are of cast iron.

33 **Ellicott Square Building, 1895–1896**
295 Main Street
Architects: D. H. Burnham and Company
Floor mosaic: 1930–1931, William Winthrop Kent of New York City
Cornice removed and exterior painted: 1971
(Detail photo shows interior of court.)

81
Downtown

This building stands on property originally reserved by Joseph Ellicott, founder of Buffalo, for his private estate. Like Burnham and Root's Rookery in Chicago, it is constructed around a large interior court. This glass-covered concourse is one of Buffalo's most ornamental public spaces. The elaborate terra cotta exterior, now painted gray, which in its essential lines follows Richardson's Marshall Field Wholesale Store in Chicago, was conceived by Charles B. Atwood (1849–1895), the designer-in-chief of the World's Columbian Exposition and master of "all artistic matters" in the Chicago-based firm of D. H. Burnham and Company. His academic French Renaissance ornamentation suffers by comparison with the imaginative detailing of Sullivan's nearby Prudential Building of the same date. When completed in 1896, the Ellicott Square Building was called the largest commercial office structure in the world.

34 Old Post Office, 1894–1901
121 Ellicott Street at South Division Street
Architects: Jeremiah O'Rourke (1894–1897), William M. Aiken and James Knox Taylor (1897–1901), with Metzger and Kent
Renovation: 1979–1981, Cannon Design, Inc.
National Register of Historic Places
(Photos show exterior, circa 1900; tower; and central light court.)

The former post office is one of the many progeny of H. H. Richardson's Allegheny County Courthouse (1884–1888) in Pittsburgh. The composition of pavilions and galleries with a tall, majestic tower and a central light court reflects the influence of Richardson's masterpiece. The skylighted central court is one of the city's most impressive interior spaces.

Before it was built, the post office became the center of a national controversy over the implementation of the Tarnsey Act (1893), the law that required architectural competitions for major federal buildings. Ranged on either side of the dispute were Daniel H. Burnham, president of the American Institute of Architects (AIA), and Henry G. Carlisle, President Grover Cleveland's Secretary of the Treasury, who, through the Office of the Supervising Architect,

controlled the erection of federal facilities. Distressed with what it regarded as the poor quality of government architecture, the AIA saw competitions as the best way to guarantee the nation good design.

Despite his assurance that the Buffalo project would be the first open to national competition, Carlisle announced in March 1894 that Jeremiah O'Rourke, the Supervising Architect, had prepared a design which had been approved. A heated exchange of letters ensued between Carlisle and Burnham, who called O'Rourke's scheme ''inferior and unworthy for the purpose.'' In the end, bureaucratic intransigence prevailed and O'Rourke's plan, modified in details, was carried to completion in 1897 by his successors, William M. Aiken and James Knox Taylor. The building has been renovated for use by the Erie County Community College.

35 Fitch House, circa 1840
159 Swan Street

This house, originally a Federal–Greek Revival with a mansard roof added later, is one of the few remaining examples of the type of residential architecture which characterized this neighborhood when Swan Street was the most important approach to the city from the east.

36 Alling and Cory, 1910–1911
136 North Division Street
Architects and Engineers: R. J. Reidpath and Son

The building is elegantly proportioned and a remarkably early use of exposed concrete frame. The "Georgian" doorcase was a regular Reidpath usage (see Gioia Industries, opposite Pierce-Arrow on Elmwood Avenue), but the classical cornice was not. Walter Gropius, in a 1913 article, used a very similar Alling and Cory building in Cincinnati, but without the architect's name, as an example for Europeans to follow.

37 Metropolitan Transportation Center, 1975–1977
181 Ellicott Street at Church Street
Architects: Cannon Design, Inc.

The Metropolitan Transportation Center combines a low-rise skylit passenger terminal with an adjoining eight-story office tower which houses the Niagara Frontier Transportation Authority. Unlike most central city bus stations, the terminal is a pleasant and even exciting space to experience, with views of travelers, buses and the city beyond afforded by comparatively large areas of glazing.

38 M&T Bank Building, 1964–1966
One M&T Plaza, Main Street at North Division
Architects: Minoru Yamasaki with Duane Lyman Associates
Plaza sculpture: Harry Bertoia

Gleaming white and stylishly slender, Yamasaki's M&T building is the most refined of the corporate monuments that have come to replace the crowded shoulder-to-shoulder street architecture of downtown. As a concession to the lost sociability of the street, lunchtime summer concerts are given in the plaza.

39 Main Place Mall–Erie Savings Bank Building, 1965–1969
Main Street at Church Street
Architects: Lathrop Douglass, mall;
Harrison and Abramovitz, bank

40 Liberty Bank Building, 1925
424 Main Street
Architect: Alfred C. Bossom
Statues of Liberty: Leo Lentelli
Addition: 1961, Duane Lyman Associates

Alfred Bossom (1881–1965) spent the years 1903–1926 in New York City, where he became a designer of skyscrapers. After that period he returned to his native England to a second career as a respected member of the House of Commons. Bossom had great faith in the skyscraper as the building of the modern age, and before he left America he wrote a book on the subject entitled *Building to the Skies*. Always a man with expansive sensibilities—Lord Bossom was renowned in London for his lavish eve-of-season partics—he generally decked out his tall buildings with romantic paraphernalia. The Liberty Bank is crowned with two reduced-in-scale replicas of Bartholdi's Statue of Liberty. High and dry above Main Street, the twin matrons form a distinctive, if slightly fantastic, feature of the Buffalo skyline. Facing east and west, they are prime symbols in the iconography of Buffalo as a city with a strategic national position. Indeed, Bossom may have remembered that Bartholdi originally envisioned his colossus at the mouth of the Suez Canal, where it was to have marked an international coming together of far-flung civilizations.

41 **Soldiers and Sailors Monument, 1882**
Lafayette Square
Architect: George Keller
Sculptor: Caspar Buberl

Lafayette Square is the second most important public space in downtown Buffalo. Originally called Courthouse Square, the area was renamed in honor of Lafayette's visit to town in 1825. Regarded by modern planners as an impediment to crosstown traffic, Lafayette Square, once a charming, parklike pedestrian area, has over the years become a thoroughfare.

The Civil War Soldiers and Sailors Monument is the work of George Keller, a Hartford architect who had a reputation as a designer of monuments. His column was erected in 1882 after enthusiasm had faded for the memorial arch by Richardson that Olmsted had proposed for Niagara Square.

42 Brisbane Building, 1895
403 Main Street, Lafayette Square
Architects: Milton E. Beebe and Son

This is the premier production of the father and son firm of local architects, Milton E. Beebe and Son, who were in demand to design churches and commercial and residential buildings in the city in the last quarter of the nineteenth century. Milton E. Beebe (1840–1922) who was a grandson of one of the first settlers in Buffalo, worked as a carpenter before setting himself up as an architect after the Civil War. His son, Henry, joined him in the 1880s.

43 Lafayette Hotel, 1904
391 Washington Street, Lafayette Square
Architects: Bethune, Bethune, and Fuchs

The Lafayette Hotel is the chief building designed by Bethune, Bethune, and Fuchs, who did many large commercial and institutional buildings in Western New York, including eighteen schoolhouses. Louise Blanchard Bethune (1856–1913), who was the first woman member of the American Institute of Architects, began her architectural career after graduating from the University of Buffalo. From 1876 to 1881 she worked in the offices of Buffalo architects Richard A. Waite (1848–1911) and F. W. Caulkins, before becoming a partner with her husband Robert Bethune.

44 Buffalo and Erie County Public Library, 1961–1963
Lafayette Square
Architects: James W. Kideney and Associates with Paul Harbach

45 Rand Building, 1929
14 Lafayette Square
Architects: Franklyn J. and William A. Kidd

46 10 Lafayette Square Building, 1958
Main Street at Lafayette Square
Architects: Emery Roth and Sons

47 **Buffalo Savings Bank, 1900–1901**
545 Main Street
Architects: Green and Wicks
Murals: Francis, Savage and Davidson
(Photo shows the Buffalo Savings Bank on the left with the Niagara Mohawk Building.)

The Buffalo Savings Bank is one of the prime examples in Buffalo of the neoclassicism inspired by the World's Columbian Exposition of 1893 in Chicago. Imperial in scale and detail, the design, which Green and Wicks prepared in competition with several other architects, effectively dramatizes a major city intersection.

The vaulted interiors, which share in the majestic spirit of the exterior, are decorated with murals depicting local history, industry, and commerce. Dominating the marmoreal banking room is the magnificent dome, bearing the signs of the zodiac within wedge-shaped fields of Renaissance ornament against a background of gold. On the pendentive representing Art appears in green-tinted grisaille a charming bird's-eye view of Olmsted's Buffalo park system, and in the deep blue oculus floats a pious motto, an opulent expression of the virtue of thrift.

48 Niagara Mohawk Building, 1912 (formerly General Electric Tower)
535 Washington Street
Architects: Esenwein and Johnson
Additions: 1924, 1927
(See photo for the preceding entry, where the building is shown at right.)

This building of gleaming white glazed terra cotta was designed by the architects who conceived the Temple of Music at the Pan-American Exposition. Inspired by the Electric Tower at the Exposition (the theme of which had been electrical power), the octagonal skyscraper crowned with a cupola echoes nineteenth-century archaeologists' reconstructions of the Pharos, the lighthouse at Alexandria, Egypt, that was one of the seven wonders of the ancient world. The imagery, which borders on kitsch, is most persuasive at night when floodlights illuminate the top of the building.

49 Market Arcade, 1892
617 Main Street
Architects: Green and Wicks
(Photos show detail of Washington Street facade and interior, circa 1900.)

A distinguished example of Beaux-Arts design, the Market Arcade is the best surviving nineteenth-century retail building in Buffalo. Intimate in scale, this charming indoor street of shops brings to mind London's Burlington Arcade, which G. B. Marshall, who financed the building, suggested to E. B. Green as a model. The building was once a shortcut from Main Street to the bustling Chippewa Market on Washington Street. With the market gone and this stretch of Main Street in the doldrums, the Market Arcade has lost its tenants. Fortunately, plans for the revitalization of the area include the rehabilitation of this single local example of a popular nineteenth-century building type.

50 **St. Michael's Roman Catholic Church, 1864**
651 Washington Street
Architect: Patrick C. Keeley

St. Michael's, which extends nearly the entire distance between Washington and Ellicott streets, was designed by Patrick Keeley, the architect who drew the plans for St. Joseph's Cathedral thirteen years earlier. Keeley, who was a favorite of Jesuit parishes like St. Michael's, endowed the church with a lively exterior of red sandstone and white limestone trim, reflecting the new popularity of color in architecture. Seriously damaged by fire in 1962, the church has a completely rebuilt interior and a diminished spire.

Reminiscent of churches in the Teutonic *Rundbogenstil*, St. Michael's served a community once predominately German. In the nineteenth century the stately church presided over the teeming Chippewa Market, which occupied the area immediately to the south. Here, in over four hundred stalls, vendors gratified the polyglot tastes of the city's many ethnic groups.

51 Shea's Buffalo Center for the Performing Arts, 1926
646 Main Street
Architects: C. W. and G. W. Rapp
Furnishings: Marshall Field & Company, Chicago
National Register of Historic Places

Shea's is today regarded as one of the finest movie palaces of its period in the country. The narrow facade belies the spacious and ornate auditorium within, which seats more than 3000 people. Originally built by Michael Shea, the theater underwent restoration beginning in 1974 by a voluntary group, the Friends of Shea's Buffalo.

52 **Calumet Building, 1906**
46–58 West Chippewa Street
Architects: Esenwein and Johnson

This is the most exuberant example of glazed terra cotta in the city.

53 **Federal Office Building, 1968–1973**
111 West Huron Street
Architects: Pfohl, Roberts and Biggie
Plaza sculpture: George Segal

54 Graystone Hotel, 1894
24 Johnson Park
Architect: Carlton Strong
Addition: 1897

This building, originally known as the Berkeley Hotel, is notable for its early use of reinforced concrete and facade of architectural concrete.

55 WGR-TV-2 Broadcast Facilities, 1969–1972
259 Delaware Avenue
Architects: Hess and Gorey
Plaza sculpture: Larry Griffis

56 Asbury United Methodist Church, 1876
80 West Tupper Street at Delaware Avenue
Architect: John H. Selkirk
Chapel: 1871

This imposing Medina sandstone church was the last and most important work of John H. Selkirk (1808–1878). Born in Litchfield, Connecticut, Selkirk came to Buffalo in 1825 and enjoyed a long career as a builder-architect. He erected many houses, churches, and commercial buildings, including the famous Tifft House, a hotel on Main Street long since demolished.

Like many Gothic Revival buildings for low-church denominations, Selkirk's church was designed with side galleries, old-fashioned features that high-church congregations had long since abandoned as uncharacteristic of medieval interiors. The original stained-glass windows were done by Booth and Reister, a local firm.

---

57 Vars Building, 1929
344–352 Delaware Avenue
Architects: Bley and Lyman

A cage for light, this Art Deco gem by local architects Lawrence Bley and Duane Lyman reduces solids to widely spaced fluted piers and three horizontal bands. The main lintel is richly decorated with geometric ornament and carries oversized consoles supporting nothing—a Mannerist conceit in twentieth-century translation.

2 West Side

No other section of the city encompasses as broad a range of neighborhoods as the West Side, from the modest nineteenth-century "workingman's cottages" of the far West Side to the post–World War I classical revival opulence of Lincoln Parkway, as that broad boulevard majestically approaches the twin neoclassical buildings of the Albright-Knox Art Gallery and the Buffalo and Erie County Historical Society Museum.

Part of the original Village of Black Rock, a separate municipality until its incorporation into the City of Buffalo in 1853, was located here. Still standing, though virtually hidden by the industrial traffic along Niagara Street, is the shell of the Union Meeting House, afterward the First Presbyterian Church of Black Rock. Built in 1828, this Greek Revival edifice, perched on the slope of Breckenridge Street overlooking the Erie Canal and Lake Erie, was the preeminent landmark in a village that at one time entertained hopes of being selected as the terminus of the Erie Canal. The village took its name from a large, projecting shelf of black basalt on the Niagara River bank near School Street, which was removed in 1825 to provide a channel for the canal. Today one still finds small, often confusing side streets on the far West Side because of the intersection of Black Rock's grid, laid out in 1802, with Joseph Ellicott's 1804 radial street system, originally designed for the village of Buffalo.

Along the streets of the lower West Side, south of Porter Avenue, it is not uncommon to see small frame and brick cottages adjacent to the more imposing homes of the affluent, for, at the time of their development, in the mid-nineteenth century, there was little of the residential segregation by class that began to characterize the city toward the end of the century. Nowadays, an older, dwindling Italian population shares the neighborhood with a young, rapidly expanding Hispanic community. The presence of Vietnamese, blacks, and native Americans combines to make the lower West Side the most heterogeneous section of the contemporary city.

The West Side includes three neighborhoods on the National Register of Historic Places: the West Village, Allentown, and Delaware Avenue historic districts. In addition, the Delaware Linwood neighborhood is listed as a city preservation district.

The West Village, adjacent to downtown, is noted for its preponderance of brick structures, evidence of the neighborhood's location within the limits of the city's fire district. Both detached Victorian residences and modest-sized apartment houses, are present here, many of them recently rehabilitated. Allentown occupies twenty-nine acres of former farmland purchased by Lewis Allen in 1829. Its main east-west thoroughfare, Allen Street, follows the original cow path running through his land from its boundary at Main Street. The area's development as a residential district occurred primarily in the 1850s and the 1860s, and its decline, as well as that of the West Village, began around the turn of the century when more spacious residential areas around Delaware Park began to attract the wealthier inner-city residents.

Extensive development of the area beyond North Street, which constituted the northern limits of the city's boundaries until 1853, did not occur until the latter decades of the nineteenth century. The booming economy of the post–Civil War era contributed to the growth of the city's middle and upper classes, who began to settle in the section now commonly referred to as the Delaware District, bounded by Richmond Avenue on the west, Linwood Avenue on the east, and Delaware Park on the north.

Richmond Avenue is, of course, an integral part of Frederick Law Olmsted's park and parkway system. The improvement of Linwood Avenue took place in the 1880s, largely through the initiative of Edward B. Smith. Smith was a

Johnson Park, West Village
St. Louis Place, Allentown, St. Louis Church in background

Argyle Park

Grant Street near Lafayette Avenue

speculative builder who often commissioned architects, such as Silsbee and Marling and F. W. Caulkins, to design dwellings here. At the juncture of Franklin and Linwood he planned a park joining the two streets into a continuous thoroughfare. This wide, tree-shaded boulevard became a street of substantial middle-class homes, and in 1886 the *Real Estate and Builders' Monthly* remarked that "beautiful Linwood Avenue bids fair to rank with Delaware as a residence street in this municipality." Today many of the late nineteenth-century houses have been recycled for medical offices.

Delaware Avenue still retains many imposing mansions, several of which are now corporate headquarters. Closer to Delaware Park itself are the comfortable enclaves of St. Catherine's Court, Argyle Park, and Penhurst Park, more intimate in scale than Delaware Avenue, but also suggestive of affluence.

In addition to the lively mix of people and neighborhoods which compose the West Side, vital commercial strips such as those along Elmwood Avenue, Grant Street, and Niagara Street are located here. The West Side is truly a microcosm of the city, and one hopes that its future will continue to reflect the rich social and architectural heritage of its past.

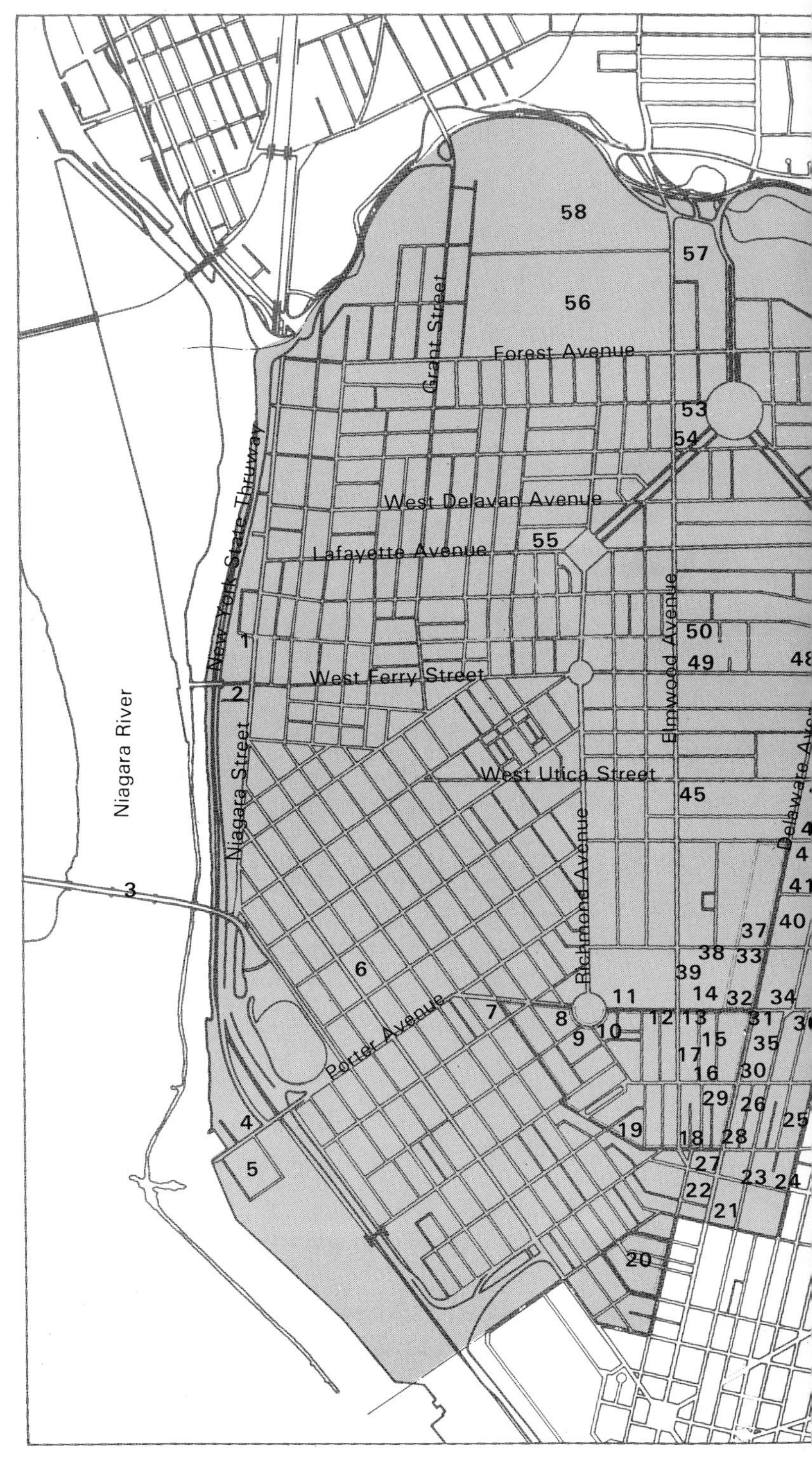

Niagara River
New York State Thruway
Niagara Street
Grant Street
Forest Avenue
West Delavan Avenue
Lafayette Avenue
West Ferry Street
West Utica Street
Richmond Avenue
Elmwood Avenue
Porter Avenue
58
57
56
53
54
55
50
49
45
1
2
3
4
5
6
7
8
9
10
11
12
13
14
15
16
17
18
19
20
21
22
23
24
25
26
27
28
29
30
31
32
33
34
35
37
38
39
40

West Side

1 First Presbyterian Church of Black Rock

2 Rich Products Building

3 Peace Bridge

4 Naval and Marine Corps Reserve Center

5 Colonel Ward Pumping Station

6 Connecticut Street Armory

7 Engine #2 Firehouse

8 Kleinhans Music Hall

9 First Presbyterian Church

10 60 Arlington Park

11 Bemis House

12 First Church of Christ, Scientist

13 Granger House

14 Mayfair Lane

15 54 Irving Place

16 Tifft Houses

17 Rohlfs House

18 Coit House

19 Coatsworth House (Cottage Street)

20 Johnson Park

21 Trinity Episcopal Church

22 Sternberg House

23 Caulkins House

24 St. Louis Church

25 McDonnell and Sons Building

26 Cary House

27 Dorsheimer House

28 The Midway

29 Cornell House

30 Twentieth Century Club

31 Theodore Roosevelt Inaugural Site

32 a.Williams-Butler House
b.Williams-Pratt House

33 Westminster Presbyterian Church

34 Episcopal Church of the Ascension

35 St. Mary's Seminary (former)
a.Drullard House
b.Freudenheim
c.Clinton House

36 North Pearl Street row houses

37 a.Clement House
b.Red Cross Blood Center

38 Spaulding House

39 E. B. Green House

40 Temple Beth Zion

41 75 Barker Street

42 Foster House

43 Campanile Apartments

44 Delaware Avenue Baptist Church

45 Elmwood Square Apartments

46 420 Linwood Avenue

47 429 Linwood Avenue

48 800 West Ferry Apartments

49 Unitarian Universalist Church

50 Chemical #5 Firehouse

51 Buffalo Crematory

52 Forest Lawn Cemetery

53 Heath House

54 Coatsworth House (Lincoln Woods Lane)

55 Lafayette High School

56 Buffalo State Hospital

57 Albright-Knox Art Gallery

58 State University College at Buffalo
a.Rockwell Hall
b.Communications Center

1 **First Presbyterian Church of Black Rock, 1828**
(now Stritt and Priebe Inc.)
44 Breckenridge Street

Built on a bluff overlooking the Erie Canal by Black Rock Methodists, Episcopalians, and Presbyterians, this building is the oldest standing church structure in the city. It is now used for commercial purposes.

2 **Rich Products Building, 1979–1980**
1150 Niagara Street
Architect: Peter Castle

A striking contemporary office building set among the older industrial structures of Niagara Street, the Rich Products building commands a spectacular view of the Niagara River.

3 **Peace Bridge, 1925–1927**
Niagara River at Front Park
Chief Engineer: Edward P. Lupfer
Consulting Engineers: William Russell Davis and John F. Stevens

The battle of Fort Erie was fought here during the War of 1812, and in 1844 Fort Porter was constructed to serve as a customs and guard house. The fort was demolished for the construction of the Peace Bridge, whose name commemorates one century of peace between the United States and Canada.

4 Naval and Marine Corps Reserve Center, 1979–1980
3 Porter Avenue
Architects: Di Donato Renaldo Associates

5 Colonel Francis G. Ward Pumping Station, 1912–1916
Porter Avenue at D.A.R. Drive
Architects: Esenwein and Johnson

The vast expanse of the engine room, and the straightforward construction have caused the interior of this building to be compared with McKim, Mead and White's Penn Central Station in New York City. At the time of its completion, the Colonel Ward station was the largest municipal pumping plant in the United States.

6 Connecticut Street Armory, 1898–1900
184 Connecticut Street at Niagara Street
Architects: Lansing and Beierl
(Interior photo shows the Grand Court.)

After Richardson's Buffalo State Hospital, the Connecticut Street Armory makes the most expressive use of native Medina sandstone of any building in Buffalo. Most impressive is the broad entrance arch with its mammoth voussoirs and deep reveals. The castle-fortress imagery was typical of such structures in the nineteenth century. The armory, which was erected on the site of the old Prospect Reservoir, contains a drill hall that at the time of construction was hailed as one of the largest unobstructed floors in the world. In addition to engineering excellence, the building possesses beautiful carved oak staircases and woodwork.

---

7 Engine #2 Firehouse, circa 1873
302 Jersey Street at Plymouth Street
Additions: 1897, 1917

The Second Empire–style Jersey Street fire station is one of the oldest firehouses in the city. Erected to serve the growing upper West Side, it shares in scale and appearance the residential character of the neighborhood.

8 **Kleinhans Music Hall, 1938–1940**
Symphony Circle, North Street at Richmond Avenue
Architects: Eliel and Eero Saarinen, with F. J. and W. A. Kidd
Acoustical consultant: Charles C. Potwin

Named by Edward Kleinhans as a memorial to his wife, Mary Seaton Kleinhans, and his mother, Mary Livingston Kleinhans, the music hall was one of the first important American commissions on which Eliel Saarinen and his son Eero collaborated. It was also one of the few such buildings erected during the Depression years. The curving shapes of the exterior, which faithfully reflect interior volumes, look forward to Eero's later architecture, while the clean lines and careful craftsmanship, evident on the interior, hark back to the elder Saarinen's devotion to Arts and Crafts ideals. Originally, the east end facing Symphony Circle was mirrored in reflecting pools which have now been filled in. Inside the music hall, the orphic form of the flaring, wood-paneled auditorium gives almost literal embodiment to Schelling's contention that architecture is frozen music.

The Saarinens' concert hall quickly gained renown for its acoustical excellence and became a place of pilgrimage for architects and acoustical engineers from all over the world. Many post–World War II concert halls show its influence, notably, Festival Hall in London (1951).

9 **First Presbyterian Church, 1889–1891**
One Symphony Circle
Architects: Green and Wicks
Tower: 1897

115
West Side

Located at the opposite end of Richmond Avenue from H. H. Richardson's Buffalo State Hospital, the Medina sandstone First Presbyterian Church clearly echoes Richardson's romantic medievalism. Its slender tower, derived from the twelfth-century church of St. Philibert at Tournus, France, majestically terminates the vista southward along one of the city's major residential thoroughfares. The vaulted and domed interior recalls St. Mark's in Venice. Stained-glass windows by Tiffany fill the end of the east transept and the choir wall and form part of an elaborate painted iconographic program devised in 1924 by William C. Francis, a local artist who was a member of the congregation. The church, which was organized in 1812, is the oldest religious body in Buffalo.

10 60 Arlington Park, circa 1867

This charming house is the best example in Buffalo of the Gothic Revival cottages that began to appear in rural and suburban America in the 1840s. Forever associated with Andrew Jackson Downing (1815–1852), who wrote much about domestic architecture and landscape gardening (and who numbered Lewis Allen among his correspondents), the board and batten cottage, trimmed with verge boards along the eaves and molded labels above the windows, was an attempt to adapt the decorative features and upright proportions of Gothic architecture to the modern dwelling. Furthermore, the vertical boarding of the exterior walls was regarded by Downing and his followers as a more honest expression of the underlying structural frame than was the traditional horizontal clapboarding. The delicately carved porch on this house, with its elaborately turned posts and reflections of Japanese taste, is a later addition, probably dating from the 1880s.

11 J. M. Bemis House, 1883

267 North Street
Architects: Silsbee and Marling

Joseph Lyman Silsbee (1848–1913), the first employer of Frank Lloyd Wright, was a Syracuse architect who in 1882 formed a partnership with James H. Marling (1857–1895) of Buffalo. Maintaining his residence in Syracuse, Silsbee continued the relationship with Marling, who was just beginning his career, until 1886 when Silsbee moved to Chicago and teamed up with another future Buffalonian, Edward A. Kent. With Marling, Silsbee designed a number of large Queen Anne houses for Buffalo, including two that appeared in *L'Architecture américaine* (1886), a French survey of building in the United States.

This house is perhaps the best work by Silsbee surviving in the city. Distinguished by inflated volumes, plunging rooflines, soaring chimney stacks, and aggressive ornament, the dwelling is typical of Silsbee's productions. The interior is finished with a variety of native woods, for Bemis was one of that vanished breed of lumber barons who made their fortunes from the rich harvest of timber from inland forests.

12 **First Church of Christ, Scientist, 1911**
220 North Street
Architect: S. S. Beman

Solon S. Beman was the architect commissioned by George Pullman to plan and supervise the construction of Pullman, Illinois. He was also a well-known designer of Christian Science churches in Chicago and elsewhere. His most prestigious commission from this denomination was for the great Mother Church (1904, with Charles Brigham) in Boston. The Buffalo edifice evokes the letter and spirit of monumental neoclassicism identified with the 1893 Chicago fair, where Beman had drawn the plans for the Mines and Mining Building and the Merchant Tailors Building. Although the latter structure directly inspired many of the churches Beman erected, his Buffalo building is based upon an original conception. The flawless Ionic portico is pleasantly scaled and so does not appear oppressive, despite its many columns. It is particularly attractive when viewed on a winter's evening bathed in the soft light of the lamps on bronze standards that flank the entrance steps.

13 E. W. Granger House, 1885

208 North Street
Architects: Green and Wicks

In 1885 the *Real Estate and Builders' Monthly* praised the ''sumptuous hardwood interiors and artistic furniture'' of this formidable house. Oak was used for the walls and ceilings of the vestibule and mahogany served to panel the reception room. A large stained-glass window by the Treadwell Studios of Boston graced the landing of the elaborate oak staircase.

The interior woodwork was from the designs of Bergen Bark, a Swedish immigrant who had studied in Berlin and Paris before working for several years with Leopold Eidlitz in New York City. In the 1880s Bark settled in Buffalo, where he took charge of creating designs for the woodworking firm of Metz, Bark, and Myer. The Granger house, which is one of Green and Wicks's first works in the city, is representative of many large dwellings in Buffalo from the 1880s and 1890s. Less than distinguished architecturally, they nonetheless possess the positive appeal of sound craftsmanship, much of which was carried out by foreign-born workmen.

14 **Mayfair Lane, 1928**
North Street between Irving and Park
Architects: Edward B. Green and Son, with Albert Hart Hopkins

Edward B. Green, Jr., who with his father designed this charming group of houses, wrote that they were built "to solve the perplexing problem of the man with a family whose interests are centered in the downtown area of the city and whose tastes run to a New England cottage nestled in the hillside, which might normally be possible in the outskirts of the city or a remote suburb." The embodiment of 1920s notions of picturesque domesticity, Mayfair Lane consists of twenty houses, erected in groups of two and four, on either side of a "street" that runs at a right angle to North Street. At the end of the lane is a diminutive manor house where lived Edward B. Green, Jr., and from which he could survey the domain he had helped to create through a window designed to look like a medieval gateway. The flagstone promenade which the houses face is elevated above a driveway (entered at North Street) that gives access to the basement level of the houses, where garages and servants' quarters are located.

121
West Side

This is architectural scenery at its most engaging. Sustained by steel girders and reinforced concrete, Mayfair Lane presents the visitors with a variety of traditional facades in wood, stucco, and brick. Modern doctrines such as ''less is more'' were thrown to the winds in the effort to create an Olde English hamlet in the midst of a modern industrial metropolis.

15 **54 Irving Place, circa 1868**

The square cupola, low-hipped roof, and entrance portico with Doric columns supporting a massive entablature are the distinguishing features of this Italianate house.

16 **Tifft Houses, 1870–1878**
149–155 Allen Street
Builder: William Tifft

This well-preserved group of brick houses exemplifies the Italianate bracketed cottage type that in the third quarter of the last century was characteristic of many middle-class neighborhoods in Buffalo.

17 **Rohlfs House, 1912**
156 Park Street
Architects: Colson and Hudson

This house is an excellent example of the Craftsman style. The client, Charles Rohlfs, a craftsman himself, was a contemporary of the Roycrofters of East Aurora, New York.

18 **Coit House, circa 1818**
414 Virginia Street
Addition: circa 1825

Here is possibly the oldest house in Buffalo, and one of its few surviving Federal ones. It was moved from its original site on the southeast corner of Swan and Pearl Streets in the 1870s, as downtown became increasingly commercial following the Civil War. In the 1960s it had become a run-down boardinghouse slated for demolition when the Landmark Society bought it and then sold it with restrictive covenants to a private owner, who has restored it.

19 Coatsworth House, 1879

49 Cottage Street

This is one of Buffalo's most impressive examples of "High Victorian," a term often used to describe late-nineteenth-century eclecticism with many volumetric projections and a strong perpendicular accent. The octagon pavilion with its wrought-iron cresting towers four stories above the street level. The coat-of-arms above the doorway suggests a continuing American deference toward European customs. Like a number of large houses close to downtown, it has passed from family to institutional ownership, and, with the urban renewal movement, back to private ownership again.

20 **Johnson Park, 1850 onward**
(Photo shows numbers 69 and 73.)

Johnson Park, a section of the West Village, is named for Dr. Ebenezer Johnson, Buffalo's first mayor, who resided in a stone Palladian villa at what is now the intersection of Johnson Park (originally Washington Park) and Delaware Avenue. His estate, which comprised 25 acres, was subdivided beginning in the early 1850s, when the roads were cut through, creating a central mall around which individual homes were constructed. Two of particular interest, numbers 69 and 73 Johnson Park, were built for Christophe Chamot, a custom bootmaker. Number 69 Johnson Park (1866), with its mansard roof, is in the Second Empire style, while 73 Johnson Park (1871) is in a Gothic cottage style. In 1911, South Elmwood Avenue was cut through the mall, and the section between Delaware Avenue and South Elmwood came to be dominated by commercial uses. The area of Johnson Park west of South Elmwood was one of the first neighborhoods in the city to be rehabilitated.

21 Trinity Episcopal Church, 1886
371 Delaware Avenue
Architect: Cyrus K. Porter
Christ Chapel: Arthur Gilman
Parish House: 1904, Cram, Goodhue, and Ferguson, who also remodeled Christ Chapel in 1913

Trinity Church was originally planned in 1869 as Christ Church. When, in the 1880s, that congregation merged with Trinity, the new parish assumed the name of the larger contingent. In 1869, after several architects, including H. H. Richardson, had submitted designs, Arthur Gilman of Boston was given the commission for a church and chapel. Only the present Christ Chapel (the small, gray stone building at the rear of the courtyard) and the foundations for Gilman's church were constructed at this time. Twenty-five years later, Çyrus K. Porter (1836–1910), a prominent local architect, reworked Gilman's plans and completed the edifice, except for the spire, which was never built.

Trinity Church possesses some of the finest stained glass in America. The five magnificent scenes in the apse and the rose window are by John La Farge, who also did several others, along with Tiffany, in the nave and transept. Especially important is his so-called Watson Window over the altar in the north transept. The subject, drawn from Revelations 7, is "The Sealing of the Twelve Tribes," a mystical event depicted in an otherworldly atmosphere of blue opalescence. The client for the window was Stephen Van Rensselaer Watson, founder of the Erie County Savings Bank, who lived across the street from Trinity in the commodious Second Empire house (1870) that is today the Buffalo Club. La Farge required that Watson allow him to exhibit the window, before sending it to Buffalo, at the 1889 Exposition Universale in Paris, where, he hoped, it would establish his international reputation as a modern master of glass. Greatly impressed by the beauty and originality of the work, the French government awarded La Farge the insignia of the Legion of Honor, the highest honor bestowed upon a foreigner.

22 **Charles F. Sternberg House, 1869–1870**
414 Delaware Avenue
Architect: George M. Allison

Architect George M. Allison, about whom little is known, designed several costly dwellings on Delaware Avenue in the 1860s and 1870s. Of the group, which included the Nims, Bell, and Altman residences, only the Sternberg house remains. Exempt from the restraint that guided H. H. Richardson in his more purely French design for the Dorsheimer house, the Sternberg house is the most characteristic example of the American Second Empire style in the city.

Sternberg, who owned a grain elevator on Ohio Street, apparently desired an abundance of light in his new home, for Allison's elevations are distinguished by many graceful, wide-awake openings. In all, there are twelve bay windows. The centerpiece of the facade is the elegant entrance porch, elevated several feet above the street. Approached by two curved flights of marble steps and trimmed with delicate iron cresting, it is supported by cast-iron Corinthian columns from which spring small pointed arches.

23 Caulkins House, 1882

415 Franklin Street
Architect: Franklin W. Caulkins

Franklin W. Caulkins, about whom little is known, was a local architect who specialized in acoustics. The *Real Estate and Builders' Monthly* noted in 1886 that he "has made a speciality of that important incident of art, for of seventeen churches which he has designed, not one has failed to be acoustically perfect." The Caulkins house is one of the best examples of Queen Anne Stick Style in the city.

24 **St. Louis Roman Catholic Church, 1886–1889**
780 Main Street
Architects: Schikel and Ditmars

St. Louis Parish, the oldest Catholic congregation in the city, was founded by Louis le Couteloux and originally served French and German immigrants. The present edifice is the third to be constructed on the site, the first having dated from 1832. Designed by a New York City firm that designed many churches throughout the east, St. Louis is one of the largest ecclesiastical buildings in Buffalo. It is built on a cruciform plan with a nave 200 feet long and a grand central tower surmounted by a 72-foot openwork spire that recalls the Gothic of J. W. Schikel's native Germany. The church organ was originally installed in the Temple of Music at the Pan-American Exposition.

25 **McDonnell and Sons Building, 1884**
858 Main Street
Builder: F. B. Gilman

This quaint little building was the office of McDonnell and Sons, who furnished the stone for numerous grave monuments in the city, including the Blocher tomb in Forest Lawn cemetery. Gilman, who was the manager of the Buffalo branch, advertised the company's product by constructing the building of granite from the firm's quarry at Quincy, Massachusetts. A gem of Neo-Grec design, the structure housed an office in the front and a sculptor's studio in the rear.

26 **Cary House, 1869**
(now More-Rubin Gallery)
460 Franklin Street

At one time, this Italianate house was the residence of George Cary, a prominent Buffalo architect, who added the wrought-iron front porch and second-story side porch.

27 **William Dorsheimer House, 1869–1871**
434–438 Delaware Avenue
Architect: H. H. Richardson
National Register of Historic Places

In October 1868 prominent Buffalo lawyer William Dorsheimer asked H. H. Richardson to design a house. This was three years after the architect had returned to America from Paris, where he had studied at the Ecole des Beaux-Arts. The Dorsheimer house closely resembles middle-class dwellings of the style known as Louis XIII, many of which were erected in the suburbs of Paris in the 1850s and 1860s. The building's simplicity and planarity, as well as the incised decoration recalling rosettes and triglyphs, undoubtedly reflect the influence of the French Neo-Grec movement. In the 1950s, the house was converted into a small office building, a transformation that effaced the original interior.

Closely associated with former U.S. President Millard Fillmore, former New York State Governor Samuel T. Tilden, and U.S. President-to-be Grover Cleveland, Dorsheimer, whose house must have been visited by each of those men, was deeply involved in local and state public affairs. As chief promoter of the park movement in Buffalo, he had invited Frederick Law Olmsted to come to the city in August 1868 to inspect a site for a large public park. Shortly before that time, Olmsted had met Richardson, for both men were members of the circle of progressive Victorian architects in New York City, and residents of Staten Island.

The Dorsheimer commission was a notable event in Richardson's career, for it led to an enduring and productive friendship. In 1877, when Dorsheimer was lieutenant-governor of New York, he succeeded in having Richardson, together with Olmsted and Leopold Eidlitz, named to complete the capitol at Albany. The Dorsheimer residence also proved to be the first of several projects in Buffalo with which Richardson became involved. In addition to the Buffalo State Hospital, first designed in 1870, and the William Gratwick house (1886–1888), which stood a few blocks north of the Dorsheimer property, at the northwest corner of Delaware and Summer, Richardson prepared designs for a number of works that were never constructed. These were churches for both Christ and Trinity Episcopal parishes (1869 and circa 1871), a Civil War soldiers' and sailors' memorial arch (1874) proposed for Niagara Square, a house for Asher P. Nichols (undated), and a library for the Young Men's Association (1884). Dorsheimer's name was associated with more than one of these underakings.

28 The Midway, 1889–1895
471–499 Delaware Avenue
(Detail photo shows 475 Delaware Avenue.)

135
West Side

This block of neoclassical row houses is unique in Buffalo for its grandeur and continuity of design. Most homeowners wealthy enough to afford houses of this class preferred to build detached dwellings, and the popularity of terrace housing common to seaboard cities did not survive here after 1850. Collectively called the Midway because the block was half the distance on Delaware Avenue between Niagara Square and Forest Lawn Cemetery, the houses were erected individually over a period of years beginning in the late 1880s on the site of the former Cornell Lead Works. The firms of Green and Wicks (477 Delaware) and Marling and Johnson (479 and 483 Delaware) were among the architects responsible for the designs. Built mostly by business and professional people, the Midway was the clearest expression in Buffalo of the genteel spirit and nostalgia for tradition that informed national taste during the so-called American Renaissance of the 1890s.

29 S. Douglas Cornell House, 1894

484 Delaware Avenue
Architect: Edward A. Kent

After study in Paris and partnership with Joseph Lyman Silsbee in Chicago, Edward A. Kent, a native of Maine, set up practice in Buffalo in the late 1880s. He designed the plans for a number of houses in the city, of which this French Renaissance design is the most impressive. One of the ill-fated passengers on the maiden voyage of the *Titanic*, Kent died at sea in 1912. Mabel Dodge Luhan, a prominent socialite and novelist, remembered him as a man with "a leaning toward beauty and lovely colors."

Cornell, who owned the Cornell Lead Works across the street from the site of the house, loved to stage amateur theatricals. For this purpose, he had Kent design a fully equipped theater in the attic story of his house. Here Cornell frequently put on performances with casts of Buffalo socialites. His granddaughter Katharine, the celebrated actress, developed her attachment for the stage from watching these productions as a young girl.

30 Twentieth Century Club, 1896
595 Delaware Avenue
Architects: Green and Wicks

From the time of Barry's Travellers' Club of 1830 in London, nearly all large social clubs chose to build their quarters in the manner of Italian Renaissance palaces. The tradition had its American monuments in the Century and University clubs in New York City by McKim, Mead and White, whose brand of neoclassicism obviously influenced Green and Wicks in the design of this building.

31 Theodore Roosevelt Inaugural Site (Wilcox Mansion), 1838
641 Delaware Avenue
Restoration: 1971, Shelgren, Patterson and Marzec
National Historic Site

The Wilcox mansion is one of Buffalo's most important historic buildings. Here, in the front parlor, on the evening of September 14, 1901, Theodore Roosevelt took the oath of office as President of the United States after the death of William McKinley, who had been shot while visiting the Pan-American Exposition.

The house itself is of considerable architectural significance, for it is the prime remaining example of the Greek Revival style in the city. Actually, the oldest part of the house, which was built around 1838, was a plain brick building used as officers' quarters for the former Poinsett Barracks and faced away from Delaware Avenue toward the parade grounds to the east. In 1845 the house was purchased by Judge Masten for his home. Masten added the portico on the Delaware Avenue side of the dwelling, making that elevation the major facade, and built a two-story wing across the back. In the mid-1890s the Gothic morning room and the classical dining room—with beautiful Georgian Revival woodwork—were designed by George Cary.

In 1966 the Wilcox house was acquired by the Department of the Interior as a historic site. Since that time much of the nineteenth-century character of the house has been restored. The front parlor or library, where Roosevelt was sworn in by his friend Ansley Wilcox, who owned the house at the time, has been returned to its appearance at the time of that event.

Delaware Avenue National Historic District

This district includes all the properties on the west side of Delaware Avenue from North Street to Bryant Street. It is also one of the city's preservation districts. Most of the nine mansions located in the area were built in the 1890s by Buffalo's rising mercantile families at a time of enormous economic expansion in the city. These venerable and stately homes have become part of a general cycle of ownership—from private, to institutional, and in many instances, to corporate, and thus back to a place on the city's tax rolls.

Typical of this trend are the two McKim, Mead and White Renaissance Revival mansions (see entry 32). The former Seymour H. Knox mansion at 806 Delaware has also undergone similar recycling. This French Renaissance house, dating from 1915–1916, was designed by the New York City architect Charles Pierpont M. Gilbert. Its Adam style music room is one of the most beautiful interior spaces in the city. The same corporate owners have purchased the Richmond-Lockwood mansion (1888), an English Tudor half-timbered manor house. The Renaissance Revival Forman-Cabana house (1894) and the Jacobean Revival Matthews house (1901) continue to serve institutional uses.

Of the three other mansions, one, the former Stephen Clement home, serves as local headquarters for the Red Cross (see entry 37). The Harlow C. Curtiss mansion (1898), by Esenwein and Johnson, now serves as the International Institute. The former Goodyear mansion (1903) is now Bishop McMahon High School. The Edward B. Green firm designed it in French Regency style for lumber magnate Charles W. Goodyear.

Descendants of some of the families who occupied Delaware Avenue homes like these and others that have given way to small office buildings and high-rise apartments tend to cling to this area, occupying smaller though substantial houses on the side streets of the old Delaware District. The closeness and convenience of a high-quality residential area to downtown Buffalo is one of the city's attractive features.

32a Williams-Butler House, 1895–1898
(now Delaware North Companies, Inc.)
Delaware Avenue at North Street
Architects: McKim, Mead and White

Built on a grand scale and costing nearly $175,000—a breathtaking sum in those days—the Williams-Butler house makes one of the best claims to palatial status of any residence in Buffalo. Expressing an ideal of formality and dignity, the stately dwelling represents that striving after good taste and domestic refinement on the European model that marked what has come to be called the American Renaissance. Distinguished by a Corinthian portico that projects from the center of a rectangular mass which is trimmed with a balustrade marking the roof, the design resembles that of the more monumental Frederick W. Vanderbilt house at Hyde Park, New York, which was also commissioned from the firm in 1895.

The plan recalls, too, that of Richardson's Dorsheimer house, with the main entrance beneath a porch on the north and the more formal facade overlooking the garden on the south. The rooms of the principal floor are disposed on either side of a broad central hall, which contains the staircase and is lit by a splendid chandelier hung from the ceiling of the upper floor.

The interior, while still impressive, is changed from White's original decorative scheme. The beamed living room, now with blond woodwork, initially displayed a more somber look. "The walls are hung in old Italian brocade," reads a nineteenth-century description. ". . . The red tones of the textile are harmonious with the dark wood of the high wainscot. At the windows are long hangings in the same rich red, and this color is reflected in the rugs."

Regarded as one of the premier residences on Delaware Avenue, the mansion, first as the home of banker George Williams and later as the residence of Edward Butler, publisher of *The Buffalo Evenings News*, was the scene of many notable events in the annals of Buffalo society. The greatest occasion planned in the house, a brilliant state dinner given by Williams for McKinley's visit to the Pan-American exposition, was abruptly canceled at the tragic news of the President's assassination.

32b **Williams-Pratt House, 1895–1896**
(now Niagara Trading Company)
690 Delaware Avenue
Architects: McKim, Mead and White

The dignified mansion for Charles H. Williams, which for many years was occupied by Jeannie Pratt, was commissioned in February 1895 and completed, at a cost of $66,700, in August 1896. As with the house next door for the client's brother, the design was put in the hands of Stanford White. He was assisted, however, by Edward York, later of York and Sawyer, well-known institutional architects.

Once enframed by luxuriant shade trees and vines and graced by a lovely garden, the house today is surrounded by more prosaic plantings and a parking lot. The handsome iron gate at the entrance was made in Buffalo by the J. H. Williams Company.

The interior has a spectacular central hall into which the grand staircase descends. Off the south side of the hall opens a conservatory. On either side of the entrance are two small rooms decorated in the Louis XV and Second Empire styles. The look throughout is opulent without being oppressive.

33 Westminster Presbyterian Church, 1859
724 Delaware Avenue
Architect: Harlow M. Wilcox
Chapel: 1940, S. Merell Clement
Addition: 1903, Tiffany Studios

This is the oldest church building beyond the old city line at North Street. The church was founded by Buffalo's first major philanthropist, Jesse Ketchum, a United Empire Loyalist who returned from Canada to live in the United States. An Italianate yellow brick structure, it looks much the same as it did when the church was first constructed, except for the Gothic pinnacles rising above the corners. In 1903 Tiffany Studios transformed the interior from Italianate to English Tudor Gothic, and extended the sanctuary 30 feet. After World War II the handsome but plain Tiffany windows were gradually replaced by the present stained-glass ones. The north side of the sanctuary depicts the Old Testament, and the south side the New. Unusual among the stained-glass windows is Henry Willet's "Praise" window on the Delaware side of the tower, which depicts Duke Ellington, Albert Schweitzer, and Charles Schultz's cartoon character, Schroeder, playing their instruments.

34 Episcopal Church of the Ascension, 1872–1873
16 Linwood Avenue
Architect: Gordon W. Lloyd
Parish House: Green and Wicks, 1920

Designed by Gordon W. Lloyd, an ecclesiastical architect from Detroit who had worked with Richard Upjohn, Ascension is a cruciform church in the Early English style of the thirteenth century, one of the favorite modes of Episcopal ecclesiologists. A 200-foot tower planned for the southeast corner of the church would have dramatized the prominent site at the head of Linwood Avenue.

35 **St. Mary's Seminary (former)**

a **Drullard House, 1862**
564 Franklin Street

Since 1884, the Solomon Drullard house, a fine brick mansard first built as a private residence, has served as the home of St. Margaret's Episcopal School (1884–1914), St. Mary's Seminary (1915–1972), and the New School of the Performing Arts (1973–1975). The building has recently been recycled as professional offices.

---

b **Freudenheim Gallery, 1867**
560 Franklin Street

This building, now an art gallery, was constructed as an addition to the Drullard house by St. Margaret's School to serve as the gym. The running track, still in place on the second level, serves as exhibition space.

c **Clinton House, 1867**
556 Franklin Street

This Italianate house was for years the home of George Clinton, a direct descendant of Governor DeWitt Clinton, who was instrumental in the construction of the Erie Canal.

36 Row Houses, circa 1885
174–182 North Pearl Street
Architect: Frederick Fischer
Renovation: 1973, Bruce Garver

37a Clement House, 1910–1913
(now American National Red Cross)
786 Delaware Avenue
Architect: Edward B. Green

To quote Henry-Russell Hitchcock's stylistic classification from the 1940 exhibition on Buffalo architecture: "An alternative to the academic classical manner of McKim, Mead and White popular in the early twentieth century was an equally academic and archeological style based on the English medieval manor house."

37b American National Red Cross Blood Center, 1977–1979

786 Delaware Avenue (behind Clement House)
Architects: Hamilton, Houston and Lownie

38 **S. V. R. Spaulding House, circa 1879**
172 Summer Street

This Italian villa–style house features a central three-story tower and bracketed eaves.

39 **180 Summer Street, 1904**
Architect: Edward B. Green

This house was designed by the architect as his own residence.

40 **Temple Beth Zion, 1966–1967**
805 Delaware Avenue
Architects: Harrison and Abramovitz
Window: Ben Shahn

The encircling wall of the temple is composed of ten scalloped panels, representing the Ten Commandments.

41 75 Barker Street, circa 1915

This is a particularly fine Colonial Revival house with end walls of masonry and a broad, six-bay facade of clapboard.

42 Orin Foster House, 1904
(now De Rose Food Brokers, Inc.)
891 Delaware Avenue
Architect: Frank H. Chappelle

This stone Italianate house with a distinct Mediterranean flavor has been renovated for commercial uses.

43 Campanile Apartments, 1929
925 Delaware Avenue
Architect: B. Frank Kelly

One of the largest and best of Buffalo's apartment houses from the pre-Depression years, the Campanile was designed by B. Frank Kelly, a Canadian who set up practice in Buffalo in 1921. In addition to this building, with its Italian Renaissance Revival details, Kelly designed a number of commercial and industrial structures.

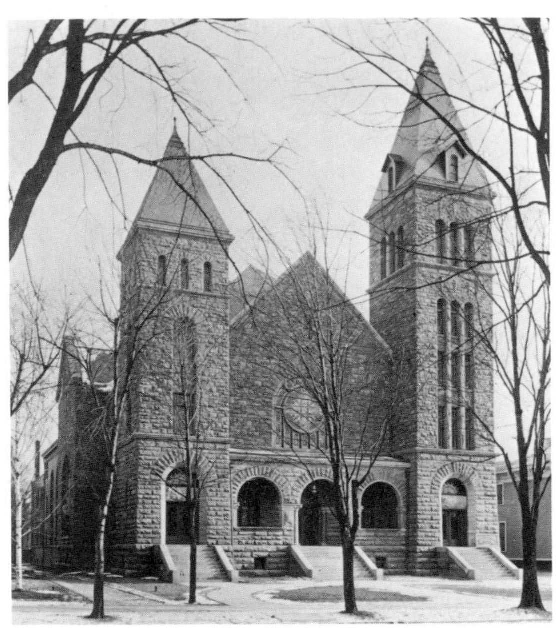

44 Delaware Avenue Baptist Church, 1894–1895
965 Delaware Avenue
Architect: John H. Coxhead

This late example of the Richardsonian idiom is the most important local building by John Coxhead (1863–1943). Coxhead, who had worked with the firm of Ware and Van Brunt in Boston, came to Buffalo in the early 1890s and practiced here for over thirty years. After that he moved to Washington, where he became Architect for the Army Air Corps.

45 **Elmwood Square Apartments, 1973**
505 Elmwood Avenue
Architects: Prentice, Chen and Ohlhausen

The design of this apartment block, sponsored by the New York State Urban Development Corporation (UDC), is based on a modular structural system developed for application throughout the state. The recessed and angled balconies give the modest-sized dwelling units a sense of spaciousness.

46 420 Linwood Avenue, circa 1885

This Queen Anne Shingle Style house, one of several on this block of Linwood Avenue, has a great sloping roof punctuated by a large tower. The roof helps to unify the great size of the house by emphasizing the horizontal plane.

47 429 Linwood Avenue, circa 1880

This house bears a strong resemblance to the Bemis house at 267 North Street, and evidence indicates that it was probably designed by the same firm, Silsbee and Marling. The wrought ironwork and the gargoyles are notable details.

48 800 West Ferry Apartments, 1929
West Ferry at Delaware Avenue
Architects: Bley and Lyman

Darwin R. Martin was the client for this project (his father, Darwin D. Martin, had commissioned the Martin house complex and the Larkin Administration Building from Frank Lloyd Wright). Along with the Campanile Apartments, 800 West Ferry constituted an attempt to popularize luxury apartment living in Buffalo, where single-family housing had long been the tradition. Two-level units, fireplaces, beamed ceilings, and large terraces were incorporated here, replicating features of the individual home in a high-rise format.

49 Unitarian Universalist Church, 1904
695 Elmwood Avenue
Architect: Edward A. Kent
Stained glass: Harry E. Goodhue of Boston

This intimately scaled church in the English Gothic style possesses an unusual hammerbeam roof structure of Maybeckian character.

50 Chemical #5 Firehouse, 1895
166 Cleveland Avenue
Architect: Edward A. Kent

One of the very few buildings in Buffalo with Art Nouveau details, the fire station was originally built to accommodate horse-drawn equipment and stables.

51 Buffalo Crematory, 1885
901 West Delavan Avenue
Architects: Green and Wicks

This is one of the best small-scale Richardsonian buildings in the city.

52 Forest Lawn Cemetery, 1850

Main entry on Delaware Avenue at Delavan Avenue
(Photos show the entranceway and the Blocher and Birge tombs.)

Forest Lawn Cemetery is an iron-fenced enclave in the heart of the city, a park in itself, complete with rolling, grassed terrain, winding roadways, large shade trees, and a reflection pond. Much of the cemetery was part of the Erastus Granger farm, Flint Hill, whose farmhouse occupied a site about where the imposing Main Street entrance arch now stands. Forest Lawn dates from 1850, but many of its graves go back before that, having been moved from earlier graveyards closer to downtown as the city expanded.

Many persons important in the history of Buffalo lie buried here, such as former U.S. President Millard Fillmore; Seneca Indian orator Red Jacket; and Pony Express partner William D. Fargo.

Because of the age of the cemetery it boasts an intriguing variety of tombstones, mausoleums, statues, and other kinds of memorials, cut from an assortment of materials, including marble, granite, and sandstone. Often these memorials reflect the architectural vocabulary of the day.

Several in particular deserve mention. One is the quaint Gothic Revival red sandstone tomb of Thomas and Amanda Crane (1853), designed by Richard Upjohn, architect of St. Paul's Cathedral

161
West Side

in downtown Buffalo and perhaps the greatest American Gothic Revival architect of the nineteenth century. Another is the handsome Renaissance sarcophagus of Francis Tracy (circa 1890), designed by Stanford White, with its cameo-like bas-relief profile of Tracy done by Augustus Saint-Gaudens.

The Blocher tomb (circa 1884) is an example of the extravagant nineteenth-century sentimentalizing of death and bereavement. A circular granite gazebo reveals the deathbed of Nelson Blocher, only son of a wealthy shoe merchant, John Blocher, who designed the statues himself. Hovering over the supine figure of the son is a granite angel, and grouped about are surviving members of the family in attitudes of sorrow.

Alongside Mirror Lake stands an example of a more restrained, neoclassical style of monument, the Birge tomb. Circled by a well-proportioned peristyle of Greek columns, open to the sky, reposes a handsome, very plain sarcophagus elevated several steps above the surrounding granite floor.

The fence surrounding Forest Lawn seems appropriate to the sense of protectiveness that one feels toward the many Buffalonians, both famous and humble, whose paths of glory or obscurity ended here at Forest Lawn.

53 William R. Heath House, 1904–1905
76 Soldiers Place
Architect: Frank Lloyd Wright
(Detail photo shows stairwell window.)

William Heath was a lawyer who served as office manager and eventually as a vice-president of the Larkin Company. Mrs. Heath was the sister of Elbert Hubbard, a former Larkin Company executive who retired in 1893 to establish, a few years later, the Roycroft Arts and Crafts community in nearby East Aurora.

The Heath commission presented Wright with the problem of situating a substantial prairie house, with its characteristically open structure, on a deep, narrow lot alongside Bird Avenue. In order to ensure a measure of privacy, Wright placed the house right up against the sidewalk (thus opening the rear of the house to a private lawn), elevated the principal living spaces well above the eye level of passersby, and treated the broad chimney, tiny entry, and stained-glass windows as screening devices. Privacy does prevail, although the splendid window patterns seem to draw attention rather than avert it.

The Heath house is a precursor to Wright's renowned Robie house in Chicago (1909) where, on a similarly narrow streetside lot, Wright struck an even more daring balance between cantilevered roofs and subtly adjusted screening mechanisms.

54 **Coatsworth House, 1897**
16 Lincoln Woods Lane
Architect: William Lansing

A copy of Richardson's famous Shingle Style Stoughton house in Cambridge, Massachusetts, built fifteen years earlier, this house was moved in two pieces in 1950 from its original site at 66 Soldiers Place to its present location.

55 **Lafayette High School, 1903**
370 Lafayette Avenue
Architects: Esenwein and Johnson

The central tower of Lafayette High School, with its mansard roof, is a neighborhood landmark.

56 **Buffalo State Hospital, 1870–1896**
(now Buffalo Psychiatric Center)
400 Forest Avenue
Architect: H. H. Richardson
Landscaping: Olmsted and Vaux
National Register of Historic Places
(Photos show north facade, south facade, tower detail, and original site plan.)

In 1864 Dr. James White, a leading physician in Buffalo, proposed to the state legislature that an asylum be established in Western New York. Largely because of his efforts, the Buffalo State Hospital organization came into existence in

167
West Side

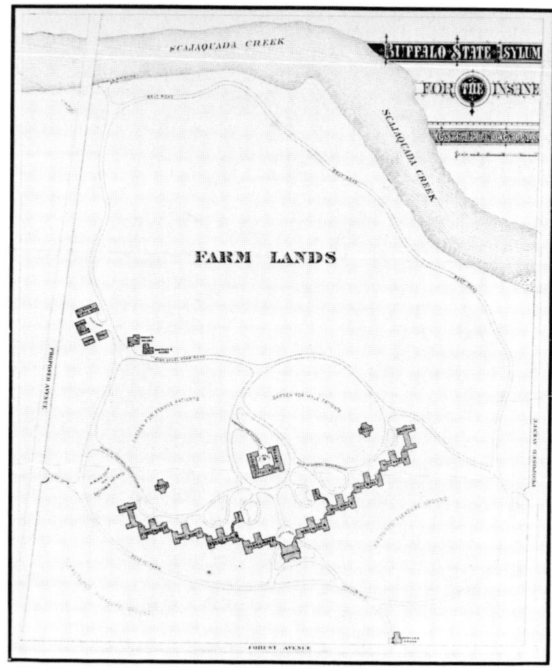

1869. In 1870 H. H. Richardson, whose office was in New York City, was chosen as architect; at the same time, A. J. Warner of Rochester was named supervising architect. Groundbreaking ceremonies took place in June 1871, and the first patients were received in the half-finished complex in 1880. The entire complex was eventually completed in 1895, nine years after Richardson's death.

Richardson's design, executed in rock-faced red Medina sandstone, is the first major example of his personal revival of Romanesque, the style with which his name is popularly identified. The hospital consisted of connected pavilions, ten in all, stretching from either side of the twin-towered administration building in the center. This building once housed officers and their families on the second and third floors, and a large chapel occupied space on the fourth floor. The five pavilions to the east (the outer three were demolished in 1969) were constructed first. Richardson wanted all of the buildings to be constructed of stone, but for reasons of economy the outer pavilions were constructed of brick, a change to which Richardson agreed.

The extended plan followed the Kirkbride system, named after the Philadelphia doctor who devised it. The plan afforded improved protection in event of fire, for each pavilion could be sealed from its neighbors by means of iron doors in the curving connecting corridors. It also provided an abundance of light and allowed for the classification of patients according to the nature and degree of their disturbance.

Frederick Law Olmsted and his partner Calvert Vaux planned the hospital grounds, which originally covered more than 200 acres. The grounds, like those of a great chateau, were both ornamental and productive. Landscaped parkland surrounded the main buildings and provided a place for quiet recreation. Behind the buildings a large tract of farmland extended to Scajaquada Creek. Here the institution grew much of its own food and provided work—considered to have therapeutic value—for many patients. The present Buffalo State College campus occupies most of the original farm.

57 **Albright-Knox Art Gallery, 1900–1905**
1285 Elmwood Avenue
Architects: Green and Wicks
Sculpture (caryatids on the east facade):
Augustus Saint-Gaudens
National Register of Historic Places
New wing: 1962, Gordon Bunshaft for
Skidmore, Owings and Merrill
(Detail photo shows caryatids on east facade.)

Planned as a temple of the arts in the tradition of many nineteenth-century museums, the Albright-Knox specifically evokes the Erectheum on the Acropolis in Athens. The handsome Ionic portico and the twin caryatid porches—with figures carved by Augustus Saint-Gaudens—derive directly from that most elegant of Greek monuments. Of the peristyle around the curved bay on the rear of the building, Henry-Russell Hitchcock said, ''rarely have Greek columns in modern times appeared more graceful.'' The chief space of the interior is the colonnaded sculpture court entered from the portico. It and the exhibition galleries were the first to employ electric lights above the skylights to ensure adequate illumination, even on Buffalo's dreariest winter days.

The art gallery was the gift of John J. Albright, a wealthy Buffalo industrialist. Edward B. Green, a close friend, also designed the Albright home, which had grounds landscaped by Frederick Law Olmsted. In 1933, after the Albright fortunes had declined, the Knox family became associated with the institution, which today houses one of the best collections of modern art in the country.

The marble and glass wing added to the south of the original building is a splendid expression of high International Style. It was designed in 1962 by Gordon Bunshaft, a Buffalonian who achieved fame in association with the office of Skidmore, Owings and Merrill. The ''black box'' houses the auditorium, while to the north is situated an open air sculpture garden, around which are grouped offices, exhibition space, and a restaurant. Sleek and restrained, Bunshaft's new wing echoes the main lines and proportions of the older building and at the same time establishes an austere contrast with its predecessor's ornateness.

58 **State University College at Buffalo**

a **Rockwell Hall, 1928**

1300 Elmwood Avenue
Architect: William Haugaard

Rockwell Hall, with its clock tower recalling Independence Hall in Philadelphia, is the centerpiece of the older portion of the State University College at Buffalo campus. This building was an early local reflection of the renewed interest in colonial architecture stirred by the reconstruction of Williamsburg, Virginia.

The Burchfield Center, a gallery which houses a collection of Charles Burchfield's paintings and specializes in the work of Western New York artists, is located here.

b **Quadrangle and Communications Center, 1967**

Architects: Perkins and Will Partnership

The new quad at Buffalo State is the best local modern example of that traditional element of college architecture. The Brutalist forms and surfaces of the buildings—students have been known to scale the elevations, pitons and ropes in hand—are most impressive in the curving masses of the Communications Center. Inside that building semi-circular lecture halls are grouped around a central court.

3 Black Rock and Riverside

Although the village of Black Rock lost its struggle with Buffalo to be chosen as the terminus of the Erie Canal, the northern part of the village, below Scajaquada Creek, did get a canal lock at the foot of Austin Street. The power generated by that lock attracted factories and flour mills. By the middle of the nineteenth century Black Rock was, after South Buffalo, the most heavily industrialized section of the city. Because Black Rock was a separate legal entity until its annexation by Buffalo in 1853, the community maintained its own water supply, marketplace, and political structure. While south Black Rock has been absorbed into the far West Side of the city, the residents of north Black Rock, many of whom are descendants of German, Polish, and other Eastern European immigrants, still retain a strong sense of their neighborhood's history of independence.

Railroads as well as the Erie Canal brought industry to Black Rock. The Tonawanda–Amherst Street intersection became one of the busiest railroad grade crossings in Buffalo. The Belt Line, a freight and commuter line with stops spaced approximately one mile apart, began operation in 1883 and created a loop of new industrial and residential communities around the city. Its impact on Black Rock's development was particularly strong.

Black Rock from the railroad tracks
Intersection of Tonawanda and Amherst Streets

Riding the Belt Line from the East Side of the city to the new urban-industrial frontier in Black Rock, hundreds of Poles began to settle on the east side of the tracks along Amherst Street. In 1888, five years after completion of the Belt Line and the expansion of Pratt & Letchworth's foundries on Tonawanda Street, Assumption Church opened. The surrounding neighborhood remains, after the Broadway-Fillmore district, the most substantial Polish community in Buffalo. St. Florian's Church, which opened in 1917 on Hertel Avenue, is a spin-off from this original settlement.

As Black Rock became increasingly industrialized, many of the younger members of families who had lived there for years began to move out. They did not want to go too far, and yet they wanted a change from the pervasive atmosphere of industry. Thus, they chose Riverside. It was here that many second- and third-generation Black Rock families were born and raised. Riverside, a short trolley-car ride from the old neighborhood, was still in an undeveloped section that offered its residents beautiful views of the Niagara River, large buildings lots, curving streets, and the ambience of suburbia.

In recent years, Black Rock and Riverside have begun to decline. The construction of the New York State Thruway in the early 1950s helped to initiate this process, by cutting off the neighborhood's access to the Niagara River, where the area's residents had fished, swum, and boated as well as worked in the mills nearby. Squaw Island, once a popular picnic ground, has been turned into a sewage disposal site by the city.

There are encouraging developments, however. The residents of Black Rock and Riverside convinced the State Legislature to build a footbridge over the Thruway to the waterfront, and have inaugurated an Annual Towpath Festival held on the banks of the old Erie Canal in celebration.

Polish Cadets Hall, Grant Street
Irene Gardner Pedestrian Bridge

Tonawanda Street
Ontario Street
14
13
12
Military Road
New York State Thruway
11
10
Amherst Street
8
9
1
2
3
7
4
6
5

Black Rock and Riverside

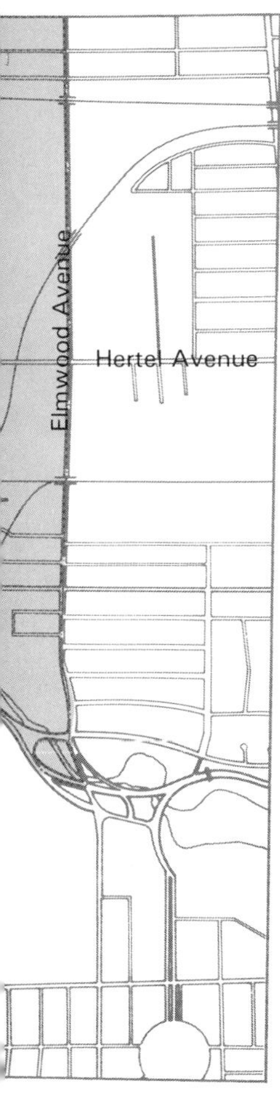

1 Black Rock Canal Lock

2 Buffalo Smelting Works (former)

3 Unity Temple

4 Customs House and Canadian National Railway Office

5 International Railroad Bridge

6 Howell House

7 St. Francis Xavier Church

8 Hook & Ladder # 12 Firehouse

9 Church of the Assumption

10 PAL Youth Center

11 St. John the Baptist Church

12 Engine #26 Firehouse

13 Chase Bag Company

14 King Sewing Machine Company

1 **Black Rock Canal Lock, 1909–1914**
U.S. Army Corps of Engineers

The lock provides passage around the swift current of the upper Niagara River to Tonawanda Harbor and the entrance of the Erie Canal.

2 **Buffalo Smelting Works (former), circa 1891**
Austin Street at Niagara River

The smelting works originally covered a large part of the area between Hamilton and Austin Streets, a center for industry and commerce because of its proximity to the Erie Canal and the locks.

3 Unity Temple, 1905
1940 Niagara Street
Architects: Green and Wicks

This Classical Revival building, flanked by a pair of Egyptian sphinxes, was built as a fraternal hall and has now been converted to a library.

4 **Customs House and Canadian National Railroad Office, 1913**
Parish Street at Dearborn

5 **International Railroad Bridge, 1873**
Niagara and Parish Streets
Engineers: Casimir S. Gzowski with E. P. Hannaford and J. Hobson

6 **Howell House, circa 1830**
189–191 Dearborn Street
Builder: Samuel Howell

This is one of the oldest extant structures in Black Rock. The stone north wing suggests the Federal style.

7 **St. Francis Xavier Roman Catholic Church, 1911–1913**
149–157 East Street
Architect: Max G. Beierl
School: circa 1893

This stately basilica church with Romanesque arches demarcating the entrance is a Black Rock landmark.

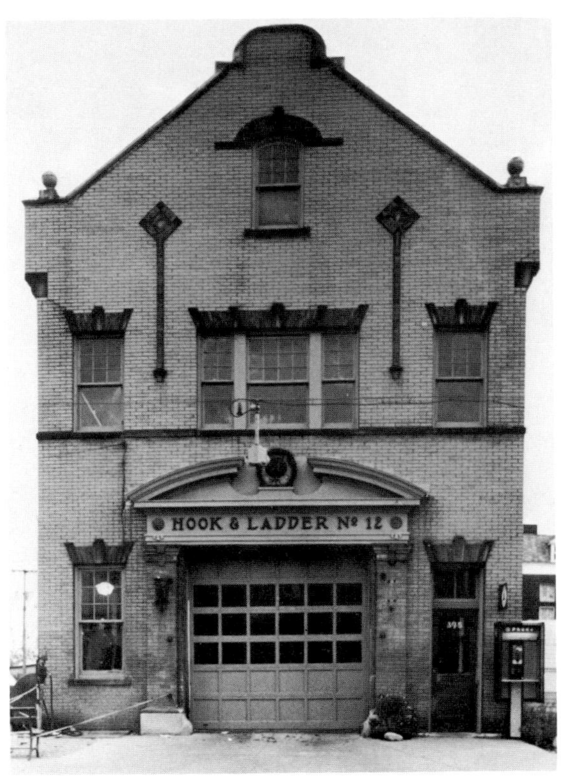

8 **Hook and Ladder #12 Firehouse, 1913**
395 Amherst Street
Architect: Howard L. Beck

9 **Church of the Assumption, 1914**
435 Amherst Street
Architects: Schmill and Gould

In its cliff-like facade, twin towers, and rose window this large, Romanesque brick church closely resembles Corpus Christi Church, which the same architects had erected in sandstone several years earlier for another Polish community on the East Side of town.

10 **PAL Youth Center, circa 1894**
346 Austin Street
Architect: Frederick C. H. Mohr
Renovation: 1979, Hamilton, Houston, and Lownie

Although the mansard roof was removed in 1954, this building, originally Police Station #13, is still notable for its wrought ironwork and masonry details.

11 **St. John the Baptist Church, 1925–1927**
60 Hertel Avenue
Architects: Oakley and Schallmo

This church gains interest from the high quality of its details rather than from the merits of its overall design. The beautiful rose window in the Italian Gothic style and the handsome Spanish Baroque portal, cast in terra cotta, are outstanding, if somewhat unoriginal features.

12 **Engine #26 Fire Station, 1894**
Tonawanda Street at Progressive Street
Architect: Frederick W. Humble

13 Chase Bag Company, circa 1890
175 Rano Street

This structure, notable for its fine brickwork details, was originally built as the C. H. Stratton Carriage Company.

14 King Sewing Machine Company, 1912
Crowley Street at Rano Street
Architects: R. J. Reidpath and Son

Window detail, Riverside United Presbyterian Church

North Park and Central Park

Although there are hints of an industrial past here, the North Park and Central Park area has always been an overwhelmingly middle- and upper-middle-class residential community. It contains substantial residences on Nottingham, Depew, Morris, and Beard, sedate tree-lined streets dotted with impressive period-revival homes in the Parkside section, and more modest one- and two-family homes on finely manicured plots on the streets adjacent to Hertel Avenue.

North Park and Central Park are dominated by Fredrick Law Olmsted's marvelous Delaware Park. It was the planning and development of what Olmsted called "the Park" in the early 1870s that stimulated the settlement of North Park and Central Park. Until then, indeed into the twentieth century, large-scale residential settlement was limited to the area south of Delaware Park.

The first section of the North Park and Central Park area to be developed was the Parkside community. In what formerly was a farm area, the streets of Parkside were laid out in the 1880s and 1890s, according to the curvilinear pattern that had become Olmsted's trademark. It was no accident that just as the city was becoming more industrialized, more ethnic—in short, more urban—Olmsted created an in-town, quasi-suburban atmosphere for the city's wealthier classes, who were seeking refuge from the changes occurring "downtown."

Following completion of Delaware Park, the Parkside Land Improvement Company, a large-scale development firm, bought up huge tracts

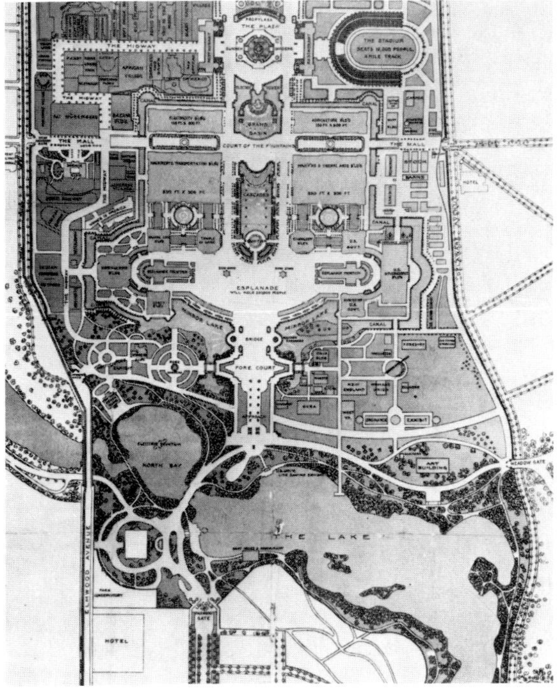

Delaware Park, the Meadow
Pan-American Exposition, 1901, plan

of land bordering the park and proceeded to subdivide it according to Olmsted's lush plans. The Sylvanus B. Nye Company performed a similar task on the west side of the North Park and Central Park area. Chosen as the site of the Pan-American Exposition of 1901, the land between the Scajaquada Creek Expressway to the south, Amherst Street to the north, and Delaware and Elmwood on either flank was not developed until the first decade of the twentieth century. At that time, the Nye Company, having bought large areas of the unimproved land from prior owners, cut out streets on the old fairgrounds, dubbed them with old English names like Middlesex and Nottingham, and thereby created in a stroke one of the most exclusive neighborhoods yet seen in Buffalo.

While large segments of North Park and Central Park were and remain upper-middle-class residential communities, whole portions, such as the Hertel Avenue section, originally developed and continue to function as zones of emergence for second- and third-generation immigrant groups. In the 1920s, as automobiles became more available and as the older East Side immigrant enclaves were beginning to decay, upwardly mobile immigrants—particularly Russian Jews (German Jews had been living in more affluent West Side neighborhoods for years)—began to move into the side streets adjacent to Hertel Avenue. During the late 1940s and early 1950s—those last few years before the massive exodus of Jews to suburbia—this was the preeminent Jewish community in Buffalo.

Although many traces of Jewish settlement can still be seen in this area (indeed, recent Russian Jewish refugees have found homes in this neighborhood), the Hertel Avenue section has become increasingly Italian and black. Hertel Avenue itself remains one of the most thriving commercial streets in Buffalo.

Although there has been change, it seems to happen at a slower, less jarring pace here than in other sections of the city. North Park and Central Park remain a bastion of family-oriented, middle-class stability.

Hertel Avenue
University Avenue

Elmwood Avenue
Delaware Avenue
Colvin Avenue
Starin Avenue
Hertel Avenue
Amherst Street
Parkside Avenue
Delaware Park
1
2
3
4
5
6
7
8
9
10
11

North Park and Central Park

1 Darwin D. Martin Complex

2 Wicks House

3 Church of the Good Shepherd

4 Russell House (former)

5 Fairfield Library

6 Beltline Central Park Station

7 Buffalo Zoo

8 Davidson House

9 Kenefick Houses

10 Buffalo and Erie County Historical Society

11 Pierce-Arrow Motor Car Company (former)

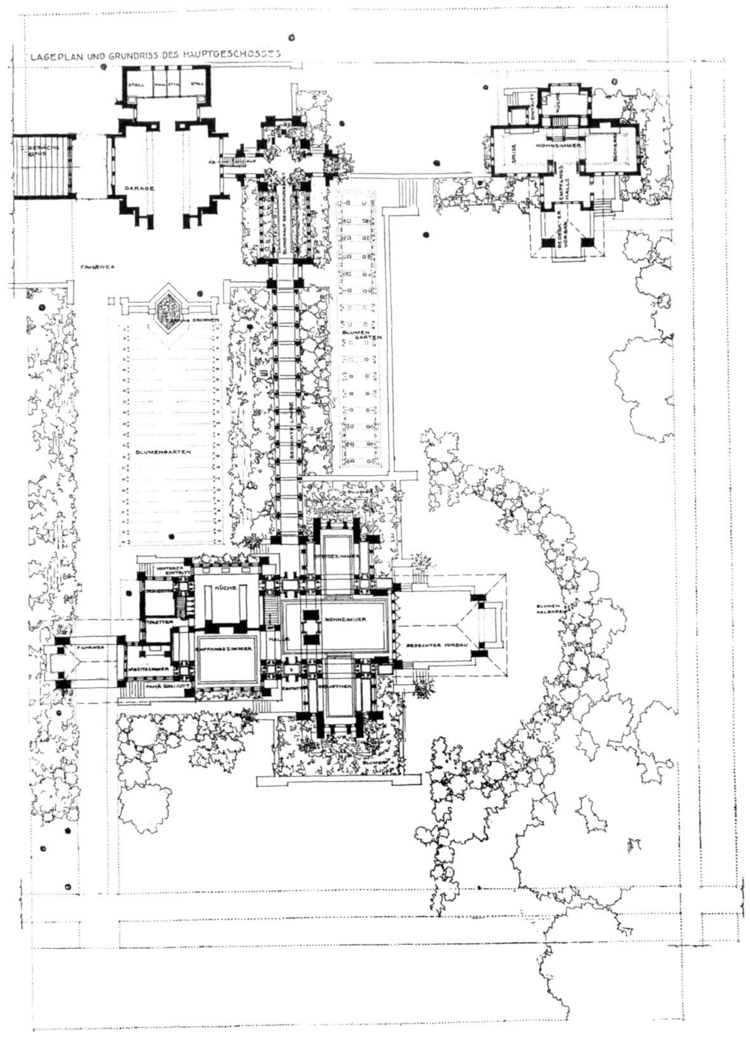

1 Darwin D. Martin Complex, 1903–1906
Architect: Frank Lloyd Wright
National Register of Historic Places
(Plan shows Barton house, Martin house, and now demolished pergola and garage.)

The complex of buildings that Frank Lloyd Wright designed for Darwin D. Martin consisted of a main house and four outlying buildings, which were unified by Wright's rigorous and consistent use of cruciform plans, piers and cantilevers, and other prairie house principles.

a **George Barton House, 1903–1904**
118 Summit Avenue

The Barton house, the first of Frank Lloyd Wright's Buffalo buildings to be completed, was built for Darwin Martin's sister, whose husband worked for the Larkin Company. The room dimensions of the house are small, but the effects of space are maximized throughout the design. The principal living spaces are concentrated in the two-story portion of the house, where the living, dining, and reception areas open freely into one another as discrete subdivisions of a continuous space. In contrast, the two major bedrooms on the second story are located at the opposite ends of a narrow corridor. Wright wrapped a continuous band of windows across the front (and rear) of the house and around the corners of these bedrooms to create an illusion of expansiveness.

The subordinate axis of the house consists of an open porch on the south with an abbreviated kitchen projecting to the north. Although this section contains very little usable living space, its function as a counterpoint to the height and mass of the two-story part of the house should not be underestimated. Wright repeatedly experimented with cross-axial plans in order to lower the profiles of his houses and extend them farther into the surrounding landscape.

b **Darwin D. Martin House, 1904–1906**
125 Jewett Parkway
Partial restoration: 1967, Edgar Tafel
(Photos show alcove detail; south facade, circa 1910; and dining room interior.)

Darwin D. Martin was the only high-ranking executive in the Larkin Company who was not related in any way to the Larkin family. His success came as the result of hard work and his invention of a card file system of accounting which revolutionized the business.

The Martin house was distinguished from most of Wright's other prairie style houses by its unusually large size and open plan. It is said that Wright was given a virtually unlimited budget for this commission.

The integrity of Frank Lloyd Wright's design is evident throughout the Martin house, from its overall plan to the detailing. This thoroughness is characteristic of Wright's organic approach to architecture. Harmony developed from his reverence for natural materials and his strict adherence to rectilinear design principles. This

consistency is apparent in the Martin house, from large-scale structural elements, to furniture, to stained-glass patterns, to millwork. The sensitive equilibrium in such a design is compromised by the loss of windows, furnishings, and the proper lighting. Originally the warm tones of fumed oak and Roman brick were augmented by gold-colored carpets, gilded masonry joints, Dutch metal wall surfaces, and soft tungsten lighting. Though modern in many of its spatial effects, the Martin house, with its aura of gilded light, owed something to the Victorian past.

Today, after periods of neglect and vandalism, the main house is partially restored, although the conservatory, pergola, and garage have been demolished. In 1954, the Martin House was subdivided into two apartments and an owner's residence, and so remained until its purchase in 1966 by the State University of New York at Buffalo. It has served as the residence for the university president, as well as headquarters for the Alumni Association and the repository for the university archives.

c **Gardener's Cottage, 1905**
285 Woodward Avenue
Additions: 1948 (first story rear); 1956 (upper story rear)

Frank Lloyd Wright strove to open up the confining "box" of traditional American houses in his prairie house designs, but the gardener's cottage, made of wood and stucco, was so modest in size that a boxy configuration appears to have been inevitable. Nevertheless, Wright managed to create an illusion of the pier and cantilever principle that characterized the Martin house by placing tall rectangular panels (or pseudo-piers) at each corner of the building.

Illusion operates inside the cottage as well. The living room extends across the entire front of the house, gathering light and a sense of spaciousness from sequences of windows on three sides. A fireplace suggests a fourth wall but allows space to extend deeper into the house on either side.

2 **Wicks House, circa 1890**
124 Jewett Parkway
Architect: William Sydney Wicks

This imposing half-timber dwelling was the home of William Wicks (1854–1919), partner of Edward B. Green (1855–1950) in the firm of Green and Wicks, Buffalo's foremost architectural office at the turn of the century. Wicks, who was born in Oneida County in central New York in 1854, trained at MIT and Cornell, where he later designed several campus buildings. In 1881 he went into partnership with Green at Auburn, New York; two years later they both moved to Buffalo, where the firm endured until 1917. In Buffalo, Wicks became a park commissioner (1897–1900) and did much to promote the Parkside community, where he lived for thirty years.

Wicks's house displayed the eclectic's love of history, as well as the verticality and boxiness of late nineteenth-century design, qualities that Wright emphatically rejected in the Martin house across the street.

3 Church of the Good Shepherd, 1888
(Ingersol Memorial Chapel)
96 Jewett Parkway
Architects: Marling and Burdett
Rectory: 1890
Children's Chapel: 1891

The original plan for this church was prepared by Silsbee and Marling. In 1888 the scheme was reworked by Marling and his new partner, Herbert C. Burdett (1855–1891), a former assistant in the office of H. H. Richardson, who, when he died prematurely, *American Architect and Building News* praised as "one of the most brilliant and successful of our young architects." The sturdy Romanesque chapel which he helped design developed from open imitation of Richardson's small libraries, especially the Ames Library in North Easton, Massachusetts. Tiffany glass fills the windows in the chancel and the children's chapel, which was added in 1891.

4 Washington Russell House, 1841
(now Dengler Funeral Home)
2540 Main Street

A distinctive feature of Buffalo architecture is the number of old farm homesteads, like this one, that survive in the city. The Russell house was originally located on a 200-acre plot of land. Other examples are the Simpson house at 638 Lafayette, the Pfohl house at 700 West Delavan, the Buffum house on Buffum Street in South Buffalo, and the old stone house at 60 Hedley Place.

5 **Fairfield Library, 1897**
1659 Amherst Street
Architect: William Sydney Wicks

The stained glass windows and choir loft are preserved inside this colonial-style building, originally constructed as the Parkside Unitarian Church and now a public library.

6 **Belt Line Central Park Station, circa 1890**
Amherst and Starin Streets

This is the last remaining station of the Belt Line Passenger Railroad, which once took passengers from one end of the city to the other for a nickel fare.

7 **Buffalo Zoo**
Main entry on Amherst Street at Colvin Street
(Photos show the Elephant House and the Aviary.)

205
North Park and Central Park

In 1875 five deer were housed in a paddock near the present zoo site. More and more grazing animals were added with the result that, in 1895, when the work became too much for the park superintendent, the city hired the first zoo curator. By the time of the Pan-American Exposition (1901), the zoo's population had risen to 270 animals.

The largest early building still in use is the Elephant House, designed by Esenwein and Johnson in 1912. The elephant head relief over the doorway is by Ira Lake. The low-profile shale limestone buildings, constructed under the Works Progress Administration in the 1930s, were designed by Henry Fruauff, and are well integrated with the landscape and outdoor animal shelters.

8 Walter V. Davidson House, 1908
57 Tillinghast Place
Architect: Frank Lloyd Wright
(Detail photos show exterior of living room bay and living room interior.)

Wright designed this house for a Larkin Company executive, Walter Davidson, who joined the company in 1906 and left both the company and the house in 1913 in order to establish the Davidson Shoe Company.

The house has a number of prairie house features in common with the Darwin D. Martin house, but its stuccoed wood construction and colorless glass are indicative of a relatively modest budget. With this in mind, Wright seems to have traded material richness for the non-material possibilities of space and light. The unobtrusive exterior of the house gives little indication of a two-story cathedral-like living room illuminated by a huge bay window at the east end of the room and by the clerestory windows along the north and south walls. West of the living room the house divides into two stories, which are in turn divided into multiple floor levels. Spatial grandeur is cleverly played off against intimacy, while even the smallest of spaces is opened up through Wright's use of banded window sequences.

Additional rooms were added to the garage in the 1930s in a manner that closely follows the style of the original house except for the arched passageway that leads through to the back yard.

57

9 **Kenefick House, 1930–1931**
51 Nottingham Terrace and 21 Meadow Road
Architect: Edmund P. Gilchrist
(Photo shows Kenefick House at right.)

Judge Daniel Kenefick had this pair of French Provincial farmhouses, both of which are white-painted brick and linked by a central courtyard, built for his sons, Daniel, Jr., and Theodore. Henry-Russell Hitchcock noted that their design indicates "how far conservative designers are coming toward a more contemporary and American style."

10 Buffalo and Erie County Historical Society Museum, 1901
25 Nottingham Court
Architect: George Cary
Addition: 1925

The masterwork of architect George Cary (1859–1945), the Historical Society building was originally erected as the New York State pavilion for the Pan-American Exposition of 1901. Built of Vermont marble, the building was the only permanent exposition structure (the others were constructed of plaster). In 1925 the building was enlarged by the addition of identical wings on the east and west sides, work that was also entrusted to Cary.

A textbook example of the neoclassicism popular after the Chicago fair of 1893, the severely Doric Historical Society quotes from the Parthenon. The handsome eight-columned portico overlooking "Gala Waters" (Olmsted's name for the lake in Delaware Park) copies, in reduced size, the Athenian temple. The sculpture in the pediment represents the forces of civilization and was carved by Charles N. Neihaus, who did the equally academic statue of Lincoln on the portico steps. Edmund R. Amateis carved the metope-like blocks above the windows depicting scenes from Western New York history.

11 **Pierce-Arrow Motor Car Company, 1906–1907**

1695 Elmwood Avenue at Great Arrow Road
Architects: Factory—Lockwood, Green & Company; Albert Kahn, Associated Architect
Administration Building—George Cary
National Register of Historic Places

George N. Pierce branched out from the manufacture of birdcages to bicycles and to automobiles in the early twentieth century. The Elmwood Avenue complex centralized all the operations necessary for automobile production, on a site previously occupied by Pan-American Exposition grounds. The company was later afflicted with various changeovers in ownership and management. That, and competition from mass-produced autombiles (the Pierce-Arrow was individually fabricated), resulted in the demise of the company in 1938. A multitude of commercial and light industrial firms now occupy the buildings on the site. Their construction exemplifies both early reinforced concrete construction and automobile plant design.

5 Kensington-Bailey

Throughout most of the nineteenth century the Kensington-Bailey area consisted of farms and timberland. Indeed, most of the territory south of Amherst Street belonged to the prosperous timber merchant William Bailey, for whom the road was named. It was the coming of the electric streetcar that changed this neighborhood, just as it did others throughout the city. The completion of the Kensington Avenue trolley line in 1895 opened up the area to the first-generation Germans who had been living in the older, more centrally located ethnic enclaves on the East Side. It was these transplanted East Side Germans who in 1902 founded St. Gerard's Roman Catholic Church, a magnificent building which continues to dominate the streetscape as well as the social life of the district.

However, it was not until after World War I that Kensington-Bailey, like North Park and South Buffalo, the other outer-ring residential neighborhoods in Buffalo, really began to develop. In all cases it was the private decision of real estate companies rather than public city planning that shaped the urban environment. A Chicago realtor named Louis Kinsey, who boasted that he had transformed a cemetery in that city into a residential community, was convinced that he could work wonders along Bailey Avenue between Delavan and Kensington. In 1919, Kinsey reported, property at the northwest corner of Kensington and Bailey was valued at $2500. One year later the same corner, to read the Kinsey Company's prospectus, was worth $25,000. The East Side, it seemed, was emptying out. In 1920 the population of the

Bailey Avenue near Kensington

Leroy Avenue, Church of the Blessed Trinity in background

Kensington-Bailey district was 18,000. Ten years later it had grown to 49,000.

Not only Germans but Poles and Italians came, too. In 1930 the last group formed their own parish on Edison Street and Roma Street: St. Lawrence's Roman Catholic Church.

What is most interesting about the Kensington-Bailey area today is that it is in a state of racial transition, and, like the lower West Side, is one of the few genuinely integrated sections of the city. Although the inner areas of Kensington-Bailey—once solidly middle-class and German—have become predominately black, the outer areas retain a delicate balance of blacks and whites.

The Kensington-Bailey district also contains the Main Street campus of the State University of New York at Buffalo. During the third decade of the twentieth century, the university began to centralize its hitherto dispersed facilities on the Main Street campus. However, by the middle 1960s state and SUNY leaders had decided to move the campus not to a downtown site, as so many Buffalonians preferred, but to suburban Amherst. This decision has not only increased the already huge task of downtown revitalization but also had an unfortunate impact on the economic health of the once vibrant commercial strip along Main Street between Bailey and Hertel Avenues. There is hope, however, that some of the damage in this area may be mended upon completion of the Main Street light rail transit line, which will extend from the foot of Main Street downtown to Bailey Avenue.

Kensington-Bailey

1 State University of New York at Buffalo, Main Street Campus

2 Bethune Hall

3 Engine #34 Firehouse

4 Trico Plant #2

5 Braun Cadillac Showroom

6 Blessed Trinity Church

7 St. Gerard's Church

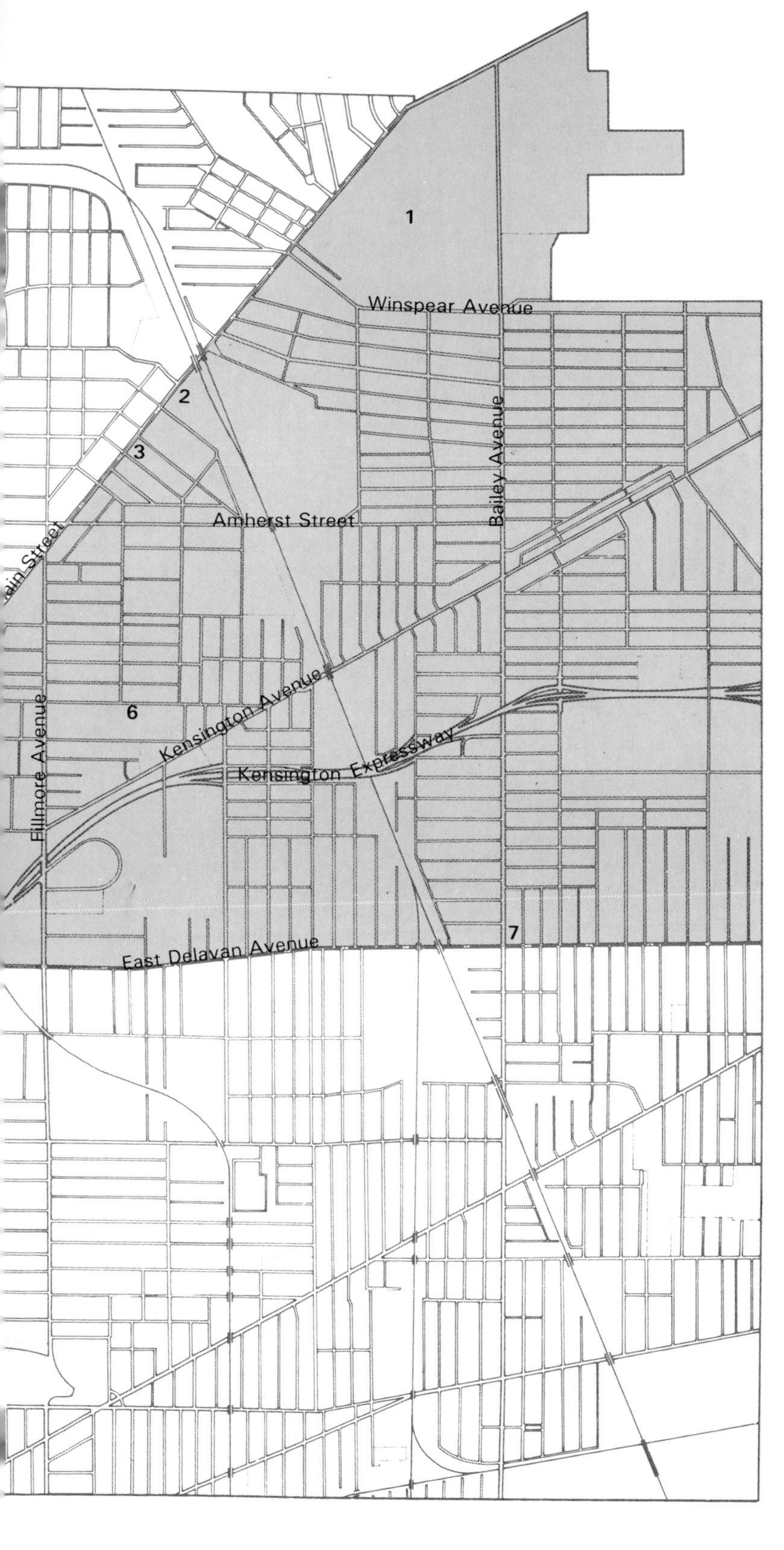

1
Winspear Avenue
2
3
Amherst Street
Bailey Avenue
ain Street
Kensington Avenue
6
Fillmore Avenue
Kensington Expressway
7
East Delavan Avenue

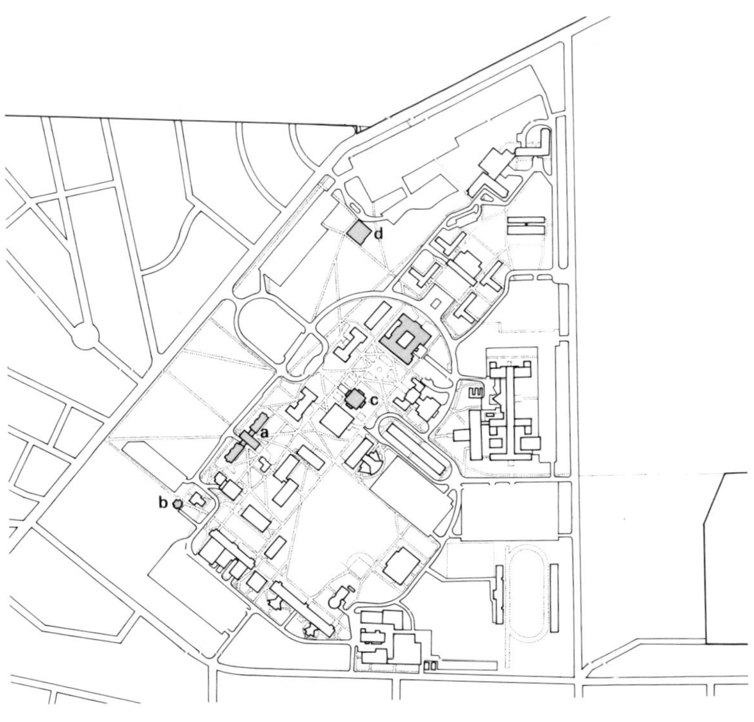

1 State University of New York at Buffalo, Main Street Campus
Main Street between Winspear and Bailey Avenue

The Main Street Campus occupies a triangular site, originally that of the old County Hospital and Almshouses. In 1909 part of the site was deeded to the University of Buffalo, which purchased the balance of the property from Erie County in 1919.

In 1922 Foster Hall, the first building to be constructed specifically for the university, was erected. Although the plan at that time was to demolish all the old hospital buildings, the former County Hospital (Hayes Hall), Maternity Home (Wende and Hochstetter halls) and Nurses' Home (Townsend Hall) still stand.

The Health Sciences and the School of Architecture and Environmental Design occupy all of the Main Street Campus. Other departments are located at the Amherst Campus.

a **Hayes Hall, circa 1865**

Hayes Hall served as a poorhouse and lunatic asylum until state regulations, passed in 1893, provided for more specialized housing for the mentally ill. It then became the Erie County Hospital, and in 1909 was acquired by the University of Buffalo. The original mansard roof and square tower were replaced in 1927, at which time the existing bell tower was constructed.

b **Beck Hall, 1931**
Architects: Edward B. Green and Son

The Faculty Club is modeled after the Holland Land Company Office (1806) in Batavia, New York.

c **Abbott Hall, 1933**
Architects: Edward B. Green and Son

d **Baird Hall, 1956**
Architect: Paul Schweikher

2 Bethune Hall, 1915
2917 Main Street
Engineers: Lockwood, Greene & Company
Addition: 1951
(Photo shows Bethune Hall at left with Bennett High School.)

Built for the Buffalo Meter Company, this most finely detailed and Bostonian of all Lockwood Greene's work in Buffalo now houses the Fine Arts Department of the State University. The original, daylit, clear-space work floors with columns at 18-foot centers survive at first- and second-story levels.

3 Engine #34 Firehouse, 1912
Main Street and Mercer
Architect: Thomas W. Harris

4 Trico Plant #2, 1915 (formerly Ford Motor Company)

2495 Main Street
Architect: Albert Kahn, with Ernest Wilby

Trico is a Buffalo-based corporation with two other plants in Buffalo. The handsome brick and terra-cotta facade of Plant #2 is not repeated in the other two buildings, but had already appeared in the Ford (now Polaroid) plant in Cambridge, Massachusetts, designed by John Graham (not Kahn or Wilby) in 1913.

5 **Braun Cadillac Showroom, 1929**
2421 Main Street
Architects: H. E. Plumer and Associates, with Harold Field Kellogg

Originally the main Pierce-Arrow showroom, this rich Art Deco design includes a remarkable tile floor with floral motifs and a coffered ceilng enriched with automobile details still visible though now painted over. The interior is best seen in the fall, when the new models are introduced and the whole elaborate lighting system is switched on.

6 Blessed Trinity Roman Catholic Church, 1923–1928
323 Leroy Avenue
Architects: Oakley and Schallmo

This extraordinary re-creation of North Italian church architecture in the midst of an otherwise nondescript neighborhood of wooden houses is the masterpiece of Chester Oakley (1893–1968), an architect prone to eclectic overkill. The dark reddish-brown brick exterior, laid in clinkers and irregular courses, faithfully mirrors the Romanesque style of Lombardy, while the interior is bright with the evocation of the Early Renaissance. The colorful terra-cotta entrance is a pastiche of the twelfth-century portal of St. Trophime at Arles, France. Oakley, about whom little is known, designed several buildings at St. Bonaventure University in Olean, New York, and was the architect of a number of Catholic churches in Buffalo in the 1920s.

7 **St. Gerard's Roman Catholic Church, 1911**
Bailey Avenue at Delavan
Architects: Schmill and Gould

Karl G. Schmill (1866–1957) had been a student of Paul Philippe Cret at the University of Pennsylvania. This handsome classical style church displays something of the refinement and elegance associated with Cret's architecture.

East Side

Buffalo's East Side was the first section of the city to become industrialized. This, more than anything else, has shaped the environment of the area. As early as the 1820s a group of entrepreneurs dammed a creek in the vicinity of Seneca and Emslie streets. Known as the Hydraulics, the area became a commercial center with a sawmill, a gristmill, and a brewery. By the 1850s, following Buffalo's railroad connection with points east and south, the East Side's future as an industrialized, immigrant, working-class community was inalterably fixed.

Choosing the East Side because of jobs, which were plentiful, and housing, which was cheap, every one of the successive ethnic groups that made their way to Buffalo settled first on the East Side. By the early 1830s blacks had established a small, tightly knit community along Michigan Avenue between Broadway and William. In 1848 the first Irish church in Buffalo was founded at Broadway and Ellicott. During the 1850s German Catholics and Lutherans became the dominant ethnic group. Settling first on Genesee, Sycamore, and Michigan, by the end of the nineteenth century they had begun to move northward to Cold Springs and the Fruit Belt. Here, on tree-lined streets with names like Peach, Lemon, Cherry, and Orange, they built more substantial homes typical of upwardly mobile first- and second-generation immigrants. The German Lutheran Seminary still stands on Maple Street, surrounded by homes built by German carpenters for themselves. The Hager Carpentry Company (1868), at the corner of Elm and William, later employed their descendants to supply the demands of the fast-growing city. Their superb woodcarving can still be found in buildings throughout the area.

The Italians came next, largely between 1900 and 1920, many of them moving in village groups: those from Campagna on Seneca and Swan streets, near downtown; those from Campo Basso and Abruzzi settled farther out, near Bailey and Lovejoy and East Delavan Avenue, respectively. Russian Jews came, too, and by 1915, Pine, Hickory, Pratt, Spring, and the other side streets between Broadway and William formed the heart of Buffalo's *shtetl.*

But by far the largest immigrant community on the East Side was the Polish. Unlike the Germans, Irish, Italians, and Jews, a great many Poles have stayed in the area. In the bustling Broadway Market, in the gigantic churches, on streets like Paderewski, along Fillmore Avenue with its host of communal organizations, there exists an ethnic community that is in many ways frozen in time.

The post–Civil War economy required unskilled labor in abundance. The Polish met this need, but in the early 1870s most were simply passing through Buffalo on their way farther west. The City Treasurer, Joseph Bork, and Father Elias Schauer, a German priest, teamed together to build a church, school and housing that would attract the immigrants to stay. In 1873, a Polish priest, Father John Pitass, was brought to Buffalo, and soon afterward St. Stanislaus Parish was founded. This was the beginning of Buffalo's large Polish settlement, which by 1900 numbered about 18,000. The influx continued throughout the early decades of the twentieth century, and the Polish presently constitute the largest European ethnic group in the city.

Paderewski Drive

Polonia Restaurant and Corpus Christi Church, from Lombard Street

Unia Polska, Fillmore Avenue

In addition to the interplay of industry and ethnicity, the physical development of the East Side has been shaped by the hand of the planner. Martin Luther King, Jr., Park is the easternmost segment of Olmsted's magnificent park system. Fillmore Avenue, like Richmond Avenue on the West Side, was designed as a boulevard linking the various components of Olmsted's park system to one another, and to the city's neighborhoods.

More recent planning decisions have done little to improve the quality of the physical environment of the East Side. The Kensington Expressway, completed in the mid-1960s, although providing a much-needed east-west intraurban arterial, was built through the heart of a pleasant, stable black neighborhood. Similar thoughtless yet all-too-typical decisions have created an uninspiring environment of high-rise public housing projects, which are a common feature of the East Side streetscape.

The East Side is today a troubled area. Despite its rich historical legacy, its future is uncertain. Because it was so heavily industrialized, the decline of industry in the city at large in recent years has had a devastating impact. Today the population is divided between a poor, young, and growing black community and a slightly more affluent, old, and shrinking Polish community. Despite the existence of still vibrant neighborhoods such as Hamlin Park, Broadway-Fillmore, and Bailey-Lovejoy, hopes for the East Side flicker, alternately brightening and dimming depending on current levels of crime, unemployment and government spending. While federal funds have led to surface improvements at major nodes, the larger impact of these programs on the more serious problems of the East Side remains to be seen.

Sycamore Street
Martin Luther King, Jr., Park

East Side

1 St. Stanislaus Church

2 Corpus Christi Church

3 New York Central Terminal

4 St. Luke's Church

5 Martin Luther King, Jr., Park

6 Buffalo Museum of Science

7 St. Francis de Sales Church

8 321 Humboldt Parkway

9 St. Vincent de Paul Church

10 60 Hedley Road

11 90 Northland Avenue

12 200–218 Glenwood Avenue

13 33–61 Emerson Place

14 St. Paul's Mall Housing

15 High Street Baptist Church

16 German Lutheran Seminary

17 Feine House

18 Metro Building

19 Courier-Express Building

20 Sidway Building

21 Burnie C. McCarley Gardens Housing

22 St. John Baptist Church

23 St. Peter's Church

24 Synagogue of the Lovers of Peace

25 Willert Park Housing

26 John F. Kennedy Recreation Center

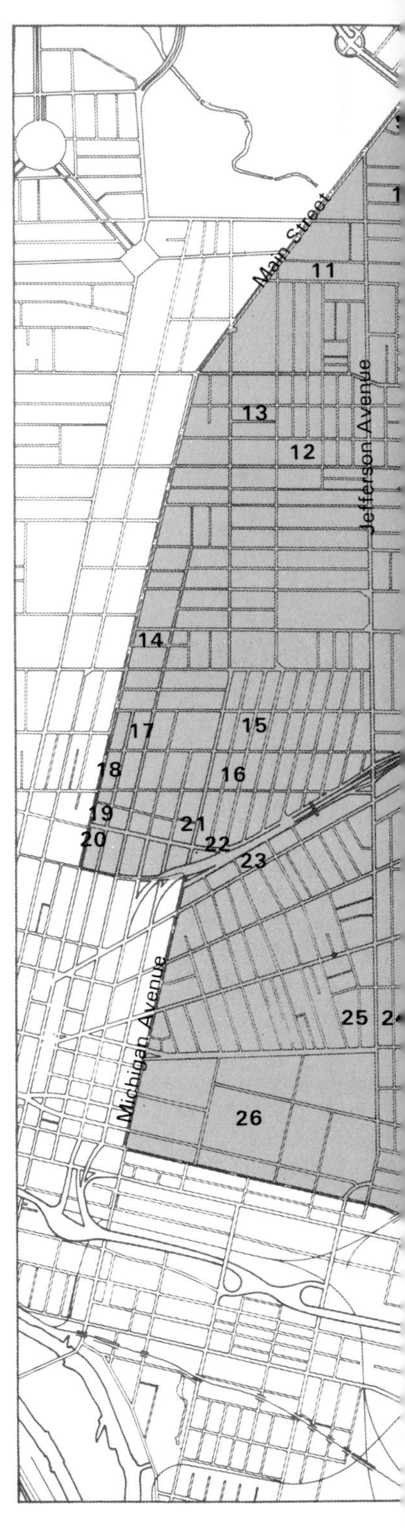

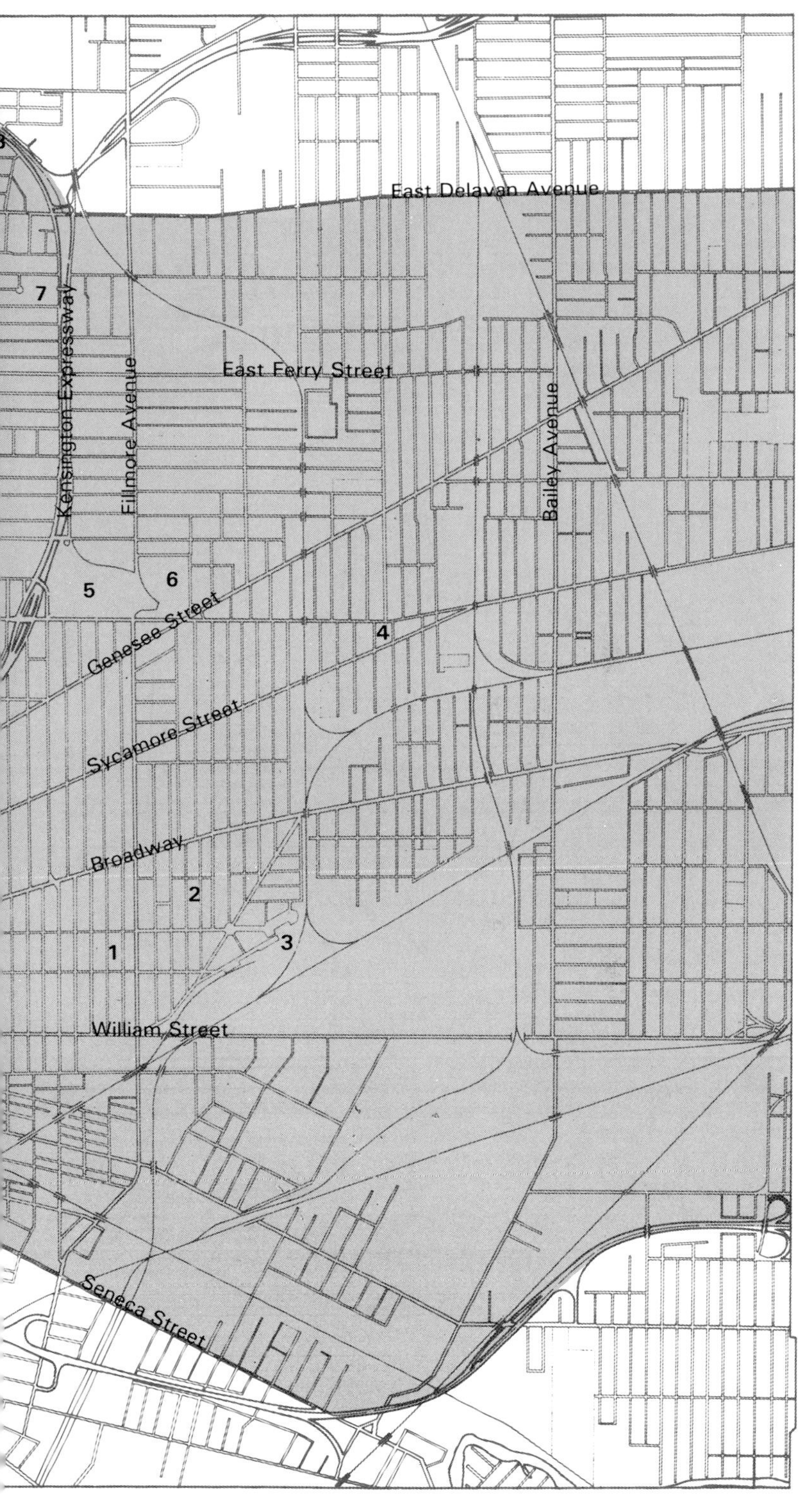
East Delavan Avenue
7
Kensington Expressway
Fillmore Avenue
East Ferry Street
Bailey Avenue
5
6
Genesee Street
4
Sycamore Street
Broadway
2
3
1
William Street
Seneca Street

1 **St. Stanislaus Roman Catholic Church, 1883–1886**

389 Peckham Street at Wilson Street
Architect: T. O. Sullivan
Towers: 1908
Restored: 1973

St. Stanislaus was the first Polish parish in Buffalo. The twin tower design of the church became a model for other churches built for Buffalo's Polish immigrants.

2 **Corpus Christi Roman Catholic Church, 1907–1909**
199 Clark Street
Architects: Schmill and Gould
Restored: 1970

This rather severe and somber exterior of dark sandstone houses an interior that is resplendent with light, color, and sculpture. The apse, with its copy of Raphael's *Disputà* in the semidome, is the focal point of this brightly painted space in which arches, vaulting, and windows are bordered with gay designs and gilded angels that look down upon the congregation from above the marbleized piers of the nave. The capitals of the nave columns were hand-carved by J. Shepperd Craig, a Scottish immigrant who settled in Buffalo in the early twentieth century and whose hand touched several churches here. In addition to the paintings and Craig's carvings, the interior of Corpus Christi was fitted with over 11,000 lights—so many that the architects thought it wise to install a generator in the basement to render the church independent of the public utility system. Lights shine not only from the chandeliers, but also along the soffits of the nave arcade and around the triumphal arch of the sanctuary.

3 **New York Central Terminal, 1929**
Memorial and Paderewski Drives
Architects: Fellheimer and Wagner
Vaulting: Rafael Guastavino Company

This is Buffalo's other Art Deco monument. Huge in scale, the terminal is even more conspicuous in its cityscape than City Hall, but is a more conventional version of the style.

Built to replace the old Exchange Street station, the Central Terminal was too far removed from downtown to be fully utilized. That fact, combined with its construction date at the start of the Great Depression, meant that this giant ''Roman bath'' complex, with its tall office tower, never realized its full potential except during World War II, when it served as a terminal for troop trains.

In recent years it has been only partially used by Amtrak. The future of this splendid East Side landmark is now uncertain, although commercial redevelopment has been proposed.

4 **St. Luke's Roman Catholic Church, 1930**
Sycamore Street at Oberlin Street
Architects: Oakley and Schallmo

The 180-foot-high campanile, octagonal baptistry, and glazed polychrome terra-cotta frieze on the main facade demonstrate the architects' preference for Romanesque tradition, also in evidence on their earlier Blessed Trinity Church (1923–1928) in the Kensington-Bailey neighborhood.

5 Martin Luther King, Jr., Park

Originally known as the Parade and later as Humboldt Park, the present park has changed greatly from Olmsted's original design for this 56-acre tract, whose function has been transformed over the years from largely ceremonial to recreational.

a **Park Shelter, 1903**
Architect: Robert A. Wallace

b **Greenhouse, 1906**
Architect: Lord and Burnham Company

6 Buffalo Museum of Science, 1929

Humboldt Parkway near Northhampton
Architects: Esenwein and Johnson

7 **St. Francis de Sales Roman Catholic Church, 1928**
407 Northland Avenue at Humboldt Parkway
Architects: Murphy and Olmstead with George Dietel

The interior of this church is noted for its fine mosaics and exquisite use of color.

8 **321 Humboldt Parkway, 1961**
Architect: Robert Traynham Coles

One of the few avowedly contemporary residential structures in the city, this house is based on the Techbuilt system of Karl Koch of Boston, with whom the architect worked in 1958–1959.

9 **St. Vincent de Paul Roman Catholic Church, 1926**
15 Eastwood Place
Architects: Thomas, Parry and McMullen
Dome: Rafael Guastavino Company

Hovering between Byzantine and Romanesque, this church by a Pittsburgh firm displays the streamlined eclecticism of the 1920s. The compact composition of masses is dominated by a saucer dome ringed with windows at the base and capped by a handsome cupola. Through the Lombard-style columned porch, one enters an interior impressive for its lofty spaces and subdued harmony of materials and ornamentation. Warm brown tones of brick and Guastavino tile in the nave and crossing act as a foil for the colorful sanctuary, with its inlaid floor and marble wainscoting, pretty baldachin, and deep blue mural entitled *The Hand of God* (by Felix Lieftucher). A superb wrought-iron chandelier suspended by a chain from the dome accentuates the air of tasteful, well-crafted opulence.

10 **60 Hedley Road, circa 1850**

This two-story stone structure, looking rather archaic in comparison with its 1890s neighbors, was built as a farmhouse in the 1850s. It later served as a part of the St. Vincent Orphan Asylum until the late 1880s, when this area of the city was subdivided for residential use.

11 **90 Northland Avenue, circa 1885**

Finely crafted woodwork enriches this modest-sized workman's cottage. Such structures as this are also often located behind single- and two-family houses in Buffalo to take advantage of the deep lots.

12 **200–218 Glenwood Avenue, circa 1890**

This row housing represents an interesting departure from the norm of detached single-family housing in the area. The wood construction lends itself to inventive detailing, including the bracketed cornice, window mouldings, and columns supporting the porch roof.

13 **33–61 Emerson Place, circa 1895**

The round bay windows of this set of row houses create a particularly impressive streetscape.

14 St. Paul's Mall Housing, circa 1910
Main Street at St. Paul's Mall
Renovation: 1975, Stieglitz, Stieglitz, Tries

Two-family housing represents about 30 percent of Buffalo's residential building stock, and is here preserved in an intact streetscape which is part of a larger urban renewal scheme for the Main Street area.

15 **High Street Baptist Church, 1883 (originally Third German Church)**
High Street at Mulberry Street

The corner site occupied by this church is dramatized by the bell tower, placed at an angle to the intersection.

16 **German Lutheran Seminary, 1854**
154 Maple Street

17 Feine House, circa 1870
(now American Lung Association)
766 Ellicott Street
Builder: John Irlbacher

August Feine, who purchased the house from John Irlbacher in 1906, was a pioneer in hand-forged wrought ironwork in the city. Originally a native of Coelleda, Germany, Feine decorated his house lavishly with examples of his trade. The fine grillwork on the front door and windows, and in particular the conservatory, which is enclosed with wrought iron, demonstrate his firm's craftsmanship.

18 Metro Building, circa 1878
855 Main Street at Virginia Street

This structure originally contained stables for the Buffalo East Side Railway Company, and was later converted to a bus depot. *(Destroyed by fire, April 1981.)*

19 **Courier-Express Building, 1930**
785 Main Street
Architects: Monks and Johnson with Henri D. A. Ganteaume

Here is a fine example of Art Deco incorporating archaic and exotic decorative motifs, in this case medieval and Celtic. The cast bronze logos and the terra-cotta reliefs on the Main Street facade display famous printers and printing processes.

20 **Sidway Building, 1907**
775 Main Street
Architects: McCreary, Wood and Bradney

This brick- and terra-cotta-clad office building, often admired for its straightforward and unpretentious design, was originally built as a four-story structure, with the two top stories added in 1913.

21 **Burnie C. McCarley Gardens Housing, 1978–1979**
Michigan Street at Goodell Street
Architect: Wallace V. Moll

22 **St. John Baptist Church, 1969**
184 Goodell Street
Architect: Wallace V. Moll

This was the first contemporary church constructed for a black parish, which also sponsored the McCarley Gardens housing project located nearby.

23 **St. Peter's Evangelical Reformed Church, 1877**
Genesee Street at Hickory Street
Architect: Milton Beebe

This Gothic-style church, with its pointed arches, tall, slender spire, and minarets, was built to serve a congregation of German settlers.

24 **Synagogue of the Lovers of Peace, 1903**
(now Church of God in Christ)
411 Jefferson Avenue
Architects: A. E. Minks and Son

25 **Willert Park Housing, 1939**
(now Alfred D. Price Housing)
Spring Street between Peckham and
William Streets
Architect: Frederick Backus

At the time of its completion Willert Park was hailed as one of the finest public housing projects in the country, for both its planning concept and architectural design. Sculptural panels by Robert Cronbach and Herbert Ambellan embellish the low-rise brick row houses and apartment buildings, which are organized around a central courtyard.

26 **John F. Kennedy Recreation Center, 1963**
114 Hickory Street
Architect: Clinton F. B. Brill

Terra-cotta detail, 512 Broadway

7 South Buffalo and South Park

South Buffalo contains some of the city's oldest settled areas. Here, along the banks of the Buffalo Creek, the Seneca Indians established a village in the 1780s, with the aid of the British, alongside whom they had fought in the Revolutionary War. Here, too, Buffalo's first white settler, Cornelius Winney, erected his log cabin. And, most important for the future urban development of the area, it was in South Buffalo that the Erie Canal terminated. No visible remnant of the Seneca Indian settlement remains, except the boulder in tiny Larkin Park on Buffum Street marking the old burial grounds. Winney's cabin is long gone. The canal, however, had a catalytic and lasting effect on the physical development of South Buffalo.

For here, at the junction of the eastern end of the Great Lakes and the western end of the Erie Canal, was located the greatest inland port of transhipment in the history of the United States. Buffalo, and more particularly, the harbor in South Buffalo, was at the geographic center of American commerce from the middle of the nineteenth to the middle of the twentieth century. Lake steamers loaded with grain, lumber, livestock, iron, and limestone docked and waited while their cargo was loaded onto canal boats and freight trains bound for the seaports of the east. Access to rail and water transportation also facilitated the development of the city's first factories. Flour mills, breweries, grain elevators, tanneries, and iron foundries all crowded the banks of the Buffalo Creek in South Buffalo.

Later economic development in the area shifted from the banks of the canal to the shores of Lake Erie. On 1000 acres of unincorporated land just outside the city, the Lackawanna Iron and Steel Company (now Bethlehem Steel), founded in 1899, began operation in 1903. By the 1920s, it was the second largest steel producer in the nation. Within the city limits, the Republic and Hanna furnaces were also established. Thus, heavy industry came to dominate, if not replace, commercial and manufacturing enterprises in and near South Buffalo.

Until the completion of the Seneca Street trolley line in the 1890s, residents of South Buffalo were confined to the cramped quarters between the downtown business district and the Buffalo Creek, sharing this little plot of space uncomfortably with factories and railroads. It was here, too, in what many of its residents still call ''the Ward,'' that the city's first immigrant group sank its roots deeply. Along Hamburg, Vincennes, Vandalia, Alabama, Louisiana, and Perry, to name but a few of the streets in the old First Ward, several generations of Irish-Americans made homes for themselves. Based partly on geography, partly on the introversion of Irish ethnicity, and partly, perhaps, on some mysterious force of urban history, South Buffalo has remained an unknown entity to many residents of other areas in the city.

By the early twentieth century the residents of the Ward had begun to spread out into South Park. With the completion of the South Park Conservatory, Cazenovia Park, and Seminole, Navaho, and Pawnee parkways, the South Park area began to assume the comfortable trappings of a quasi-suburban, middle-class community. However, South Park's development also replicated many features of the old First Ward, such as rows of two- and three-family homes, the predominance of Irish parishes, like that of Holy Family Church, and the prevalance of dozens of social and political clubs. Thus, many of South Buffalo's mid-nineteenth-century characteristics remain intact, and, seemingly, if the majority of the people who live there have it their way, not much will change in the future.

Buffalo Creek
Elk Street in the old First Ward

McMurphy's Ginmill, Seneca Street
Mullin's Barbershop, Seneca Street

South Buffalo and South Park

1 Larkin Company Complex (former)

2 Grain Elevators

3 Tifft Farm Nature Preserve

4 Holy Family Church

5 Liberty National Park

6 South Park Conservatory

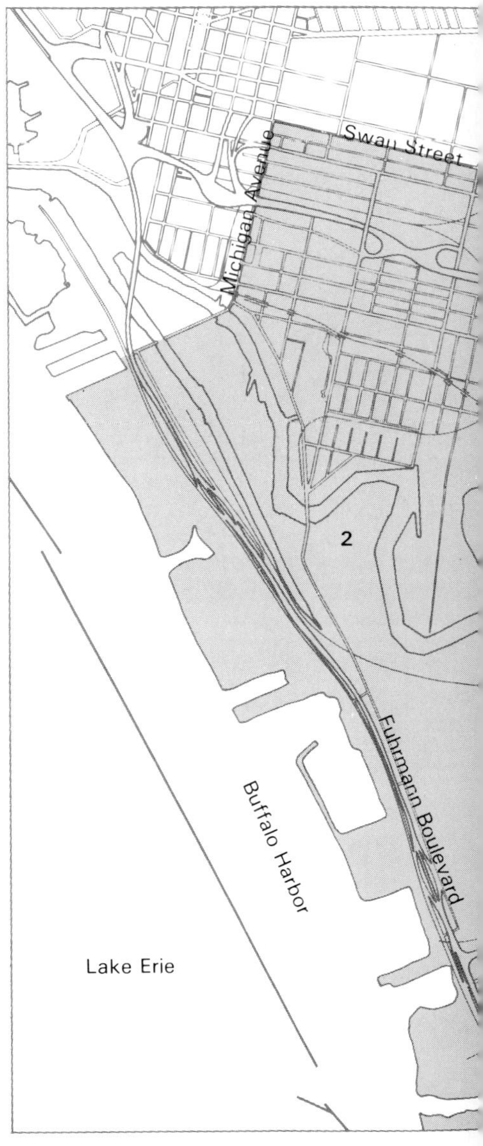

1
Seneca Street
New York State Thruway
Elk Street
Clinton Street
Buffalo River
Abbott Road
5
Cazenovia Park
4
Tifft Street
Hopkins Street
South Park Avenue
McKinley Parkway
South Park
6

---

1 **Larkin Company Complex (former), 1896–1913**
Seneca Street at Larkin, Van Rensselaer, and Hydraulic Streets

Even without Frank Lloyd Wright's Larkin Administration Building (a fragment remains at the back of the parking lot by the Swan Street railroad bridge), this is still one of the most important historic industrial sites in the United States, and one of the biggest, with almost 2,000,000 square feet of usable floor space still intact.

The powerhouse, between the railroad bridge and Larkin Street, and the ''L'' and ''M'' warehouses on the back of it, are all of 1902–1904 by the Reidpath office. The carefully detailed, brick-arched construction, which can be seen on the ''L'' and ''M'' warehouses, was the idiom of all the main facades of those parts of the complex which were of brick and steel mill-construction. The facades of the gigantic block known now as 701 Seneca, running from Larkin to Van Rensselaer Streets, were modernized in the early 1950s. Behind the stucco and the false flat transoms of the facade, however, everything was in the regular Reidpath idiom, except for the 1913 rebuilt ''C'' building on the rear (Carroll Street) facade, where the three bays of reinforced concrete frame give a vivid demonstration of the gain in window area derived from the switch to framed construction.

The design for the rebuilding of ''C'' was made in house, but clearly follows Lockwood, Greene's system for the ''R, S, T'' warehouse (otherwise the terminal warehouse) at the back of the complex, between Van Rensselaer and Hydraulic Streets. Designed in 1911, built by the Aberthaw Construction Co. in just over six months in spite of its great size, a brilliantly conceived packaging and shipping facility, ''R, S, T'' has long been recognized as a masterpiece of functional design and rational detailing. It has been commendably maintained by its present owners, Graphic Controls, who also added the ''Wrightian'' entrance on Exchange Street in 1969, by Arthur Carrara.

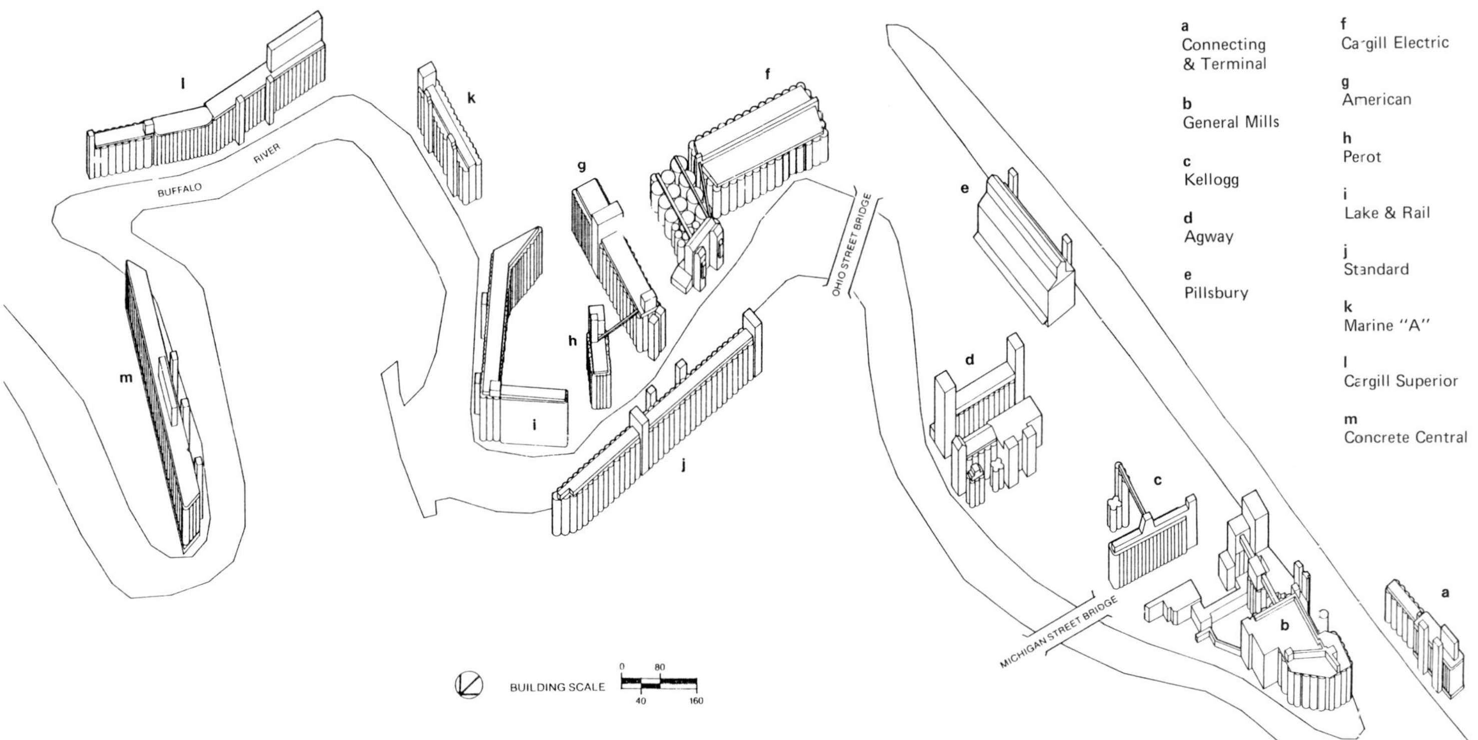

a
Connecting
& Terminal
b
General Mills
c
Kellogg
d
Agway
e
Pillsbury
f
Cargill Electric
g
American
h
Perot
i
Lake & Rail
j
Standard
k
Marine "A"
l
Cargill Superior
m
Concrete Central
OHIO STREET BRIDGE
MICHIGAN STREET BRIDGE
BUFFALO
RIVER
BUILDING SCALE
0
80
40
160

2 Grain Elevators
Buffalo River

Buffalo is regarded as having the best historical collection of elevators extant, and all the significant examples, bar one, are concentrated in one area. The straggler is the Pillsbury, on Ganson Street, a wasteland once lined with elevators on both sides. The rest are on Kelly Island, all along the reach of the Buffalo River that is spanned by the Ohio Street Bridge and bordered by St. Clair Street and Childs Street. The most monumental of all, Concrete Central, can be seen from the foot of Childs, but cannot be reached now except by water or a long safari on foot from South Park. Visitors should console themselves by going to the foot of St. Clair Street and turning right along South Street far enough to look back toward the Ohio Street Bridge, down an architectural perspective composed entirely of grain elevators, but so grand that it has been called the finest urban prospect in Buffalo.

Having originated in Minneapolis, the cylindrical concrete bins that make up these monumental structures are not a Buffalo invention. (The earliest, from 1906, are now buried in the middle of the General Mills plant.) The basic mechanism of the elevator—the "marine leg," which reaches down to elevate the grain from the holds of the ships—did, however, originate here with Joseph Dart's elevator of 1842, and marine legs, either mobile or "stiff," are a conspicuous feature of all Buffalo's riverside elevators. Through a remarkable series of historical accidents, a disproportionately large number of Buffalo elevators were illustrated in European publications between 1913 and 1930, another reason why Buffalo is often considered to be the "elevator capital" of America.

e Pillsbury Elevator, 1898
Ganson Street
Engineer: Max Toltz, with D. A. Robinson, Architect
Builder: James Stewart & Company

Built by the Great Northern Railroad, and long known as the Mutual Elevator, this reputedly is the last of the "brick box" type still operational in North America. The monumental exterior brick walls are a pure weather barrier, the grain being stored in an independent system of steel bins inside. The four-story "head house" is also an independent structure, steel-framed, hung from the top of the walls. Marine towers are replacements for the originals, toppled by a hurricane in the early 1920s.

f **Cargill (Electric) Elevator, 1897**
Childs Street
Builder: Steel Storage and Elevator Construction Co.

The steel parts constitute the oldest (probably first ever) all-electric elevator in the world, and the workhouse and marine legs are unique. The 1940 concrete addition by H. G. Onstad, which runs along the river side to the Ohio Street Bridge, appears from outside to be a conventional cluster of cylinders; they are, in fact, half-cylinders used to form a powerful self-buttressing wall around six gigantic open bins, each 150 × 90 feet at the base and soaring to a height of 80 feet.

j **Standard Elevator, 1928**
St. Clair Street
Builder: James Stewart and Co. with A. E. Baxter, Architect

Baxter was responsible for the architectural side of many major elevators in Buffalo; the Standard is the most accessible. It is done in his characteristic manner, with the self-conscious addition of architectural details in the first phases (nearest the Ohio Street Bridge) and the stern omission of such details in the later (1942) "functionalist" phase. The well-kept "garden" setting is also notable and worth viewing from the other end of St. Clair Street.

3 **Tifft Farm Nature Preserve, 1973–1976**
1200 Furhrmann Boulevard

This 264-acre environmental education center includes six miles of trails. Originally an Indian hunting ground, and later a manmade port, the property became a dumping ground before the development of Tifft Farm. The location provides spectacular views of South Buffalo's industrial landscape from within the nature preserve.

4 **Holy Family Roman Catholic Church, 1906**
1885 South Park Avenue
Architect: Lansing and Beierl

The predominately Irish-American parish of Holy Family was established in 1902 as one of the first Catholic churches in the South Park area. The interior of the church is appropriately embellished with ornament adapted from the Book of Kells.

5 Liberty Bank, 1921
2221 Seneca Street
Architect: Harold Jewett Cook

Originally the South Side Bank of Buffalo, the building displays detailing inspired by the ornament of Louis Sullivan.

6 South Park Conservatory, 1898
South Park Boulevard and McKinley Parkway
Architects: Lord and Burnham Company
Addition: 1929, Howard L. Beck

The great popularity which public conservatories enjoyed in the late nineteenth century dates from Joseph Paxton's design for the Crystal Palace (1851) in London. Its assembly utilized prefabricated iron structural members and glass panels, a technique which lent itself to mass production and rapid construction. Greenhouse manufacturers such as Lord and Burnham were quick to adopt this technology, ideally suited to their specialized requirements. The South Park Conservatory originally contained five greenhouse structures, since expanded to fifteen.

Like other cities, Buffalo has lost a disquieting number of important buildings. Some were casualties of economic and social changes, some of changes in architectural fashions, and others of our pragmatic penchant for measuring progress and quality of life almost completely by standards of utility and modernity. The intention here, however, is not to analyze the reasons for the disappearance of these buildings but to record some of the significant and interesting ones now gone from the Buffalo scene.

Any vanished building designed by a famous architect or architectural firm should be included as part of local and national architectural history. Buffalo has lost buildings by Frank Lloyd Wright, H. H. Richardson, and McKim, Mead and White.

Another category of lost buildings is that of houses of famous people who lived in Buffalo. There was, for example, the Millard Fillmore house, a Gothic Revival crenelated and towered mansion which stood on Delaware and Niagara Square where the Statler Hotel now holds sway. There was also the Mark Twain house on the west side of Delaware just above Virginia, a handsome Italianate house in which Twain lived from about 1869–1871 while he was editor of the Buffalo *Express.* And there was the towering mansard mansion of William D. Fargo of Wells-Fargo Pony Express fame. Built during the years 1868–1870, with a center pavilion rising to five stories, it occupied a park-like area complete with fountain and gardens that covered the whole acreage from Fargo to West and from Pennsylvania to Vermont streets. It was taken down in 1890, giving way to the many smaller homes that now occupy the site.

Three other large estates which were enclaves in themselves—principalities or dukedoms within the city—were those of General Peter B. Porter, Bronson Rumsey, and John J. Albright. These properties, too, gave way to the exigencies of public transportation, the space needs of an expanding population, and changes in the circumstances of their owners.

The Porter Mansion (1816), later the Porter-Lewis Mansion, was an early stone Federal house, later considerably remodeled. It stood with its several outbuildings on the embankment at Niagara and Ferry overlooking an imposing, orchard-filled slope which extended all the way down to the Niagara River. A hero of the War of 1812, General Porter was later this area's first congressman, and afterwards secretary of war in John Quincy Adams's cabinet. It was at this home that General Lafayette, John Quincy Adams, and DeWitt Clinton were entertained when they came to Buffalo. Lewis Allen, uncle of Grover Cleveland and the owner of the farm which gave Allentown and Allen Street their names, bought the home in 1836 and lived in it until his death in about 1890. It was here that Grover Cleveland made his home when he came to Buffalo.

The Bronson C. Rumsey estate, called Rumsey Park, built about 1865, embraced all the land westward from Delaware and Tracy to about what is now Whitney Place. Perhaps the first French Second Empire or mansard house erected in Buffalo, it overlooked at its rear a picturesque, spring-fed lake replete with a Swiss chalet boathouse, a Greek temple pavilion, terraced gardens, fountain, and woodland paths. In the moonlight it must have looked like an Albert Pinkham Ryder painting. The extension of Elmwood Avenue cut through part of the grounds and began the gradual partition of the estate.

The John J. Albright estate also occupied a beautiful, park-like tract of land, designed by Frederick Law Olmsted. The property was on Ferry Street just west of Delaware, extending through to Cleveland Avenue. When the original house burned in 1901, it was replaced by a magnificent stone Tudor Gothic mansion, designed by the firm of Green and Wicks. A victim of the Depression era, it was torn down about 1935, and the estate was subdivided for residences less opulent, but nevertheless intended for upper-income families.

One of the most important Greek Revival houses in Buffalo was the Ellicott-Goodrich-Glenny-Hoyt mansion, which originally stood on the corner of Main and High streets. It was begun in 1823 by the surveyor-planner and founder of the city, Joseph Ellicott, who also designed the house. Because of his ill health and then his death in 1826, he was never able to complete it. Colonel Guy H. Goodrich finished it in 1831 and occupied it for many years. About 1899 the University of Buffalo Medical Department bought the land, and John C. Glenny bought the house, had it moved in sections, and rebuilt and enlarged on an Amherst Street site just west of the present Nichols School soccer field. About 1910 William B. Hoyt bought it and also enlarged it. Noted Buffalo architect George Cary designed both additions. It was torn down in 1946 to make way for the United Church Home. In 1940 Henry-Russell Hitchcock referred to it as "long the finest house in Buffalo."

Among the interesting commercial buildings Buffalo has lost is the Erie County Savings Bank Building (1893–1967) at Church and Franklin streets. Constructed of brown sandstone, it was one of the last buildings in Buffalo to employ solid masonry construction. Its architect, George B. Post, followed a Richardson Romanesque style, especially in the medieval corner turrets and the groupings of four stories of windows under tall arches, as in Richardson's famous Marshall Field Wholesale Store in Chicago.

Also now demolished are two major cast-iron-front buildings located in downtown, the German Insurance Company (1875–1957) on Lafayette Square and Main Street and the Tucker Building (1877–1977) on Court near Pearl Street.

Among the notable public buildings that have disappeared is the Federal Building, known also as the Old Customs House (1858–1965) on the corner of Washington and Seneca Streets. Designed by Ammi B. Young, the supervising Architect of the U.S. Treasury Department, it was, according to Henry-Russell Hitchcock, "a refined adaptation of Renaissance palace architecture to the uses of a growing democracy."

William D. Fargo House

Shelton Square, showing the Erie County Savings Bank Building (right), St. Paul's Episcopal Cathedral, and the Prudential Building

The German Insurance Company
Pierce's Palace Hotel

Other old buildings whose passing might be noted with nostalgic regret are Old Fort Porter, whose Tintern Abbey-like romantic Gothic ruins were removed in 1925 to make way for the approach to the Peace Bridge; the unbelievable, Disney-World towered and mansarded Pierce's Palace Hotel (erected in 1877 and almost completely destroyed by fire in 1881), which stood on Prospect Avenue about where the main D'Youville College Buildings are now; entertainment centers, such as Elmwood Music Hall, the Old Teck, and the Century Theater; the old tanneries and breweries that contributed much to the economic life of Buffalo; numbers of fine churches located downtown; and several imposing railroad stations downtown, notably the neoclassical Lehigh Valley on Main Street, where the General Donovan Office Building now stands, and the Delaware, Lackawanna and Western Terminal on the Buffalo River at the foot of Main Street. Finally, some precious open space in the city has been lost here and there or otherwise encroached upon. A certain amount of Frederick Law Olmsted's park system, for example, has been sacrificed for Peace Bridge facilities and expressways.

The Larkin Administration Building, 1904–1906
(demolished 1950)
680 Seneca Street at Swan
Architect: Frank Lloyd Wright
Client: John D. Larkin, Sr.
Sculpture: Richard Bock
(Detail photos show skylit court, reception desk, and original metal furniture.)

Frank Lloyd Wright designed the Larkin Administration Building in 1904 to accommodate the 1800 corresponding secretaries, clerks, and executives of this once flourishing mail-order company, whose manufacturing buildings still exist just across Seneca Street from the site of the Wright building. The Larkins needed a clean and comfortable building in order to attract first-rate (chiefly female) employees to an otherwise industrial section of the city. Wright's numerous innovations contributed significantly to this objective. Clean air was distributed throughout the sealed interior of the building from a rudimentary air-conditioning system in the basement. Metal office furniture, built-in file cabinets, wall-hung toilets, and a gracious restaurant and conservatory all contributed to the ambience of the building and were featured as part of daily factory tours.

Today the Larkin Administration Building is universally regarded as a landmark in the development of modern architecture. Its unadorned exterior surfaces were shaped according to the individualized functions they enclosed. For instance, the paired forward towers contained stairways and air-intake shafts for the air cleaning system. The articulation of the side elevations was a direct expression of the structural framework of the building.

A solitary surviving brick pier at the edge of the site provides some indication of the scale, material, and color of this lost masterpiece.

James F. Metcalfe House, 1882–1884
(demolished 1980)
125 North Street
Architects: McKim, Mead and White

By the summer of 1882, when the Metcalfe house was commissioned, McKim, Mead and White had already built a number of suburban houses based on their perception of American colonial architecture. In 1895 Russell Sturgis published an extended review of their accomplishments up to that time and singled out the Metcalfe house as an example of "the less academical and more spontaneous . . . picturesque country buildings" which the firm had designed. By that time, however, McKim, Mead and White had abandoned this line of domestic architecture and espoused the monumental neoclassicism typified by the two Williams houses that still stand at North and Delaware.

In the exterior design of the Metcalfe house one saw reflections of seventeenth- and eighteenth-century American dwellings. The steeply pitched gabled roof projecting beyond the walls, the shingles covering the gables and the curved bay on the side, the coved facade cornice, and the asymmetrical arrangement of the openings all harked back to that earlier period. Yet the ample proportions, plate glass panes, deep veranda or "piazza" on the front, the mixture of stone and brick for the walls, and the provision of a separate service wing at the rear of the house were expressions of nineteenth-century usage.

By a stroke of good luck, the superb woodwork of the principal interiors survived in excellent condition, despite the fact that for many years the building served as a boardinghouse. All was carefully removed before demolition and donated to institutions in New York City and Buffalo. The paneled hall and parlor, together with the staircase, were given to the Metropolitan Museum of Art to be reconstructed in its American wing. The dining room and library went to Buffalo State College, and several large mantelpieces were donated to the Buffalo and Erie County Historical Society.

William H. Gratwick House, 1886–1888
(demolished 1919)
776 Delaware Avenue
Architect: H. H. Richardson

The William H. Gratwick house stood at 776 Delaware Avenue at the northwest corner of Delaware and Summer. It was Richardson's last commission, according to his biographer Mariana Van Rensselaer, before he died in 1886. A heavy, brownstone Romanesque building, it was finished by the firm that continued Richardson's practice—Shepley, Rutan and Coolidge.

Robert Keating Root House, 1896
(demolished 1935)
Delaware and North Streets
Architects: McKim, Mead and White

The Robert Keating Root house stood on the southwest corner of Delaware and North, where a Howard Johnson restaurant now stands. The large, handsome, Colonial Revival mansion bore some resemblance, on a smaller scale, to the McKim, Mead and White–designed Eastman House in Rochester.

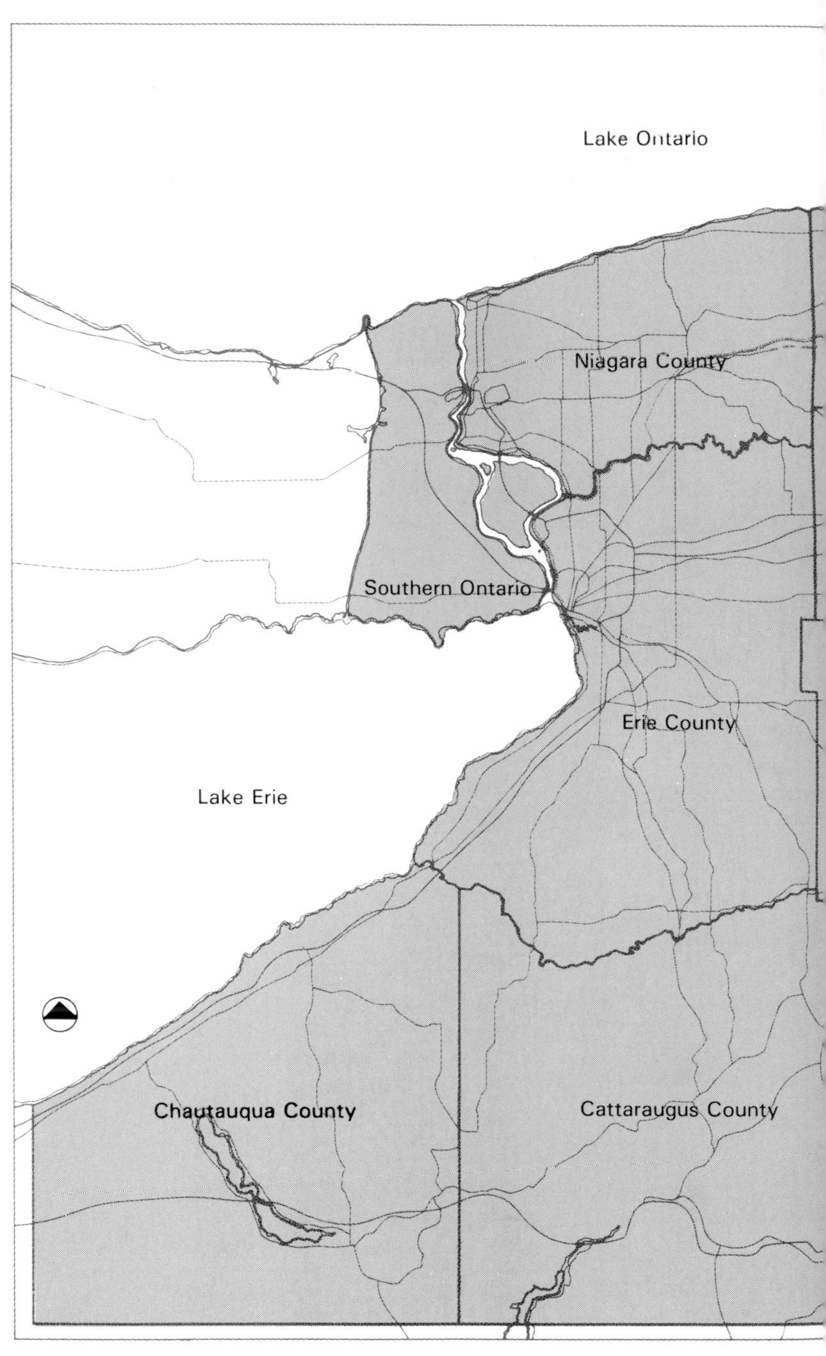
Lake Ontario
Niagara County
Southern Ontario
Erie County
Lake Erie
Chautauqua County
Cattaraugus County

Western New York and Southern Ontario

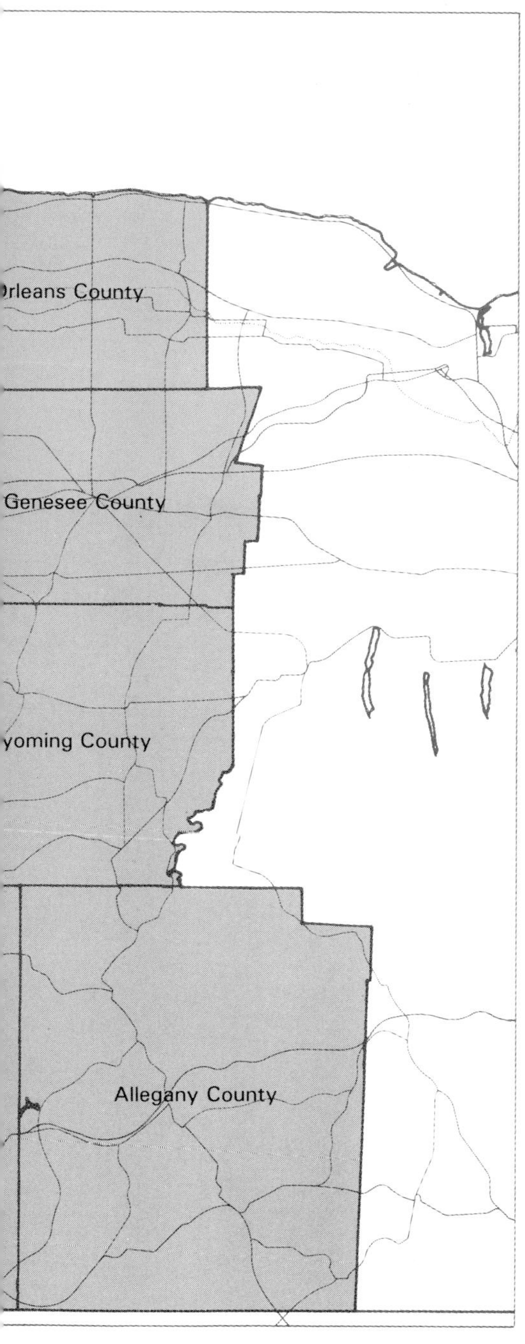

9 Erie County

Although the focus of this book is on Buffalo architecture, the city must be presented in context. Buffalo is within Erie County; is, with Niagara County, part of the Niagara Frontier; is fifteen miles from Niagara Falls and just across the river from southern Ontario; and is part of an eight-county region known as Western New York. Sharing the Niagara River and the Erie Canal has given Buffalo, Erie County, and Niagara County close historical affinities. Much of the richness of being a Buffalonian derives from Buffalo's proximity to these other areas. Many Erie County residents, especially those living in towns near Buffalo's corporate limits, call themselves Buffalonians. The brief descriptions that follow will help acquaint the reader with Buffalo's surroundings.

The forty towns and villages in Erie County show a great diversity of architectural work. Almost every building type is included in a rich visual panorama that continually reminds us of the variety as well as the excellence of our nineteenth-century architectural heritage. Vernacular buildings include more than a dozen log cabins dating from the beginning of the nineteenth century. The oldest of these is the log cabin near Bowmansville (circa 1800).

One of the most picturesque structures is also the oldest continually operating business of the county. The 1811 Williamsville Water Mills is two miles off the Thruway, where it overlooks historic Glen Park and Ellicott Creek. The 1871 Village Meeting House, now the Williamsville Historical Society, is a stone's throw away. Williamsville, important in the War of 1812, also retains several structures built of the local Onondaga limestone. Among these are the oldest church in Western New York still used for services, the 1834 Mennonite Church on Main Street, and also the Mill Street houses near the creek. A few miles north are the two sites of the growing Amherst Old Colony Museum Park, a broad assemblage of early settlers' buildings containing exhibitions of related artifacts and crafts.

In the town of Lancaster, the 1894 Central Avenue Town Hall Opera House has undergone major restoration. Nearby are fine Queen Anne, Georgian, and Gothic Revival homes of wood and brick and, southeast, the carefully restored Little Red Schoolhouse of 1868. In adjoining Cheektowaga, on Union Road, stand the elaborately detailed Maria Hilf Chapel and the comfortably spacious Hitchcock and Urban houses, representative of the preferences of the community leadership of early times. These northeast communities include the Asa Ransom house on East Main Street, Clarence, a nationally known and sensitively restored inn-restaurant. Farther east are the 1848 Charles B. Rich octagon house at Akron, and a part-cobblestone house on Four Rod Road in Alden.

To the north of Buffalo, in the City of Tonawanda, the early regional lumber capital of Erie County, the architectural traveler comes upon the Long homestead (1829) on the Erie Canal and the Old Railroad Station museum (1870). The St. Peter's Church museum (1849) and Albert Kahn's celebrated Chevrolet factory (1937) are found in the Town of Tonawanda. The Richardsonian Medina sandstone Eberhardt mansion (1894) is one of the landmarks of the Village of Kenmore. To the west on the west shore of historic Grand Island in the Niagara River stands Riverlea, the Lewis Allen summer home, where Allen's nephew Grover Cleveland often came in the summer. Adjacent to Beaver Island State Park, it is now the headquarters of the Grand Island Historical Society.

Driving in any of the southerly towns of Erie County, the traveler will discover architectural charm enhanced by the scenic beauty of the Boston Hills. Indeed, Eden calls itself the "Garden Spot of Western New York." Its early residential neighborhoods include the Asa Warren house (circa 1840) and the 1848 Coach Stop Inn restaurant on Main Street, both restored.

The neighboring villages of Orchard Park and East Aurora are especially rich architecturally. In Orchard Park, the 1820 Quaker Meeting House on East Quaker Road exemplifies the sturdy character of its founders, as Dr. Jolls's Italianate house (circa 1869) expresses the taste and influence of leading citizens. "Edgewood" on the Jewett-Holmwood Road has been called the "best Greek Revival house in Western New York." On Shearer Street in East Aurora President Millard Fillmore's cottage of 1826, a National Historic Landmark, has recently undergone beautiful restoration. Elbert Hubbard's Roycroft Campus at Main and Grove Streets is acclaimed nationally for the honest assemblage of a variety of craftsman's structures. The Roycrofters produced some of the best achievements of the American Arts and Crafts Movement. The Roycroft Institute represented a protest against the dehumanizing effects of the Industrial Revolution. It was an American relative of the Pre-Raphaelite Movement and of William Morris's "feudal" colony in England. Today, the campus still has active craftspeople and includes a restaurant, crafts shop, and museum.

Griffin's Mills, several miles outside East Aurora on either side of Mill Road, is an architectural repository of early nineteenth-century building. Gone is the mill itself, once picturesquely sheltered by the ageless shale gorge of Cazenovia Creek. But several fine old buildings survive, notably the Paul-McCormick house (circa 1820), perhaps the finest Federal frame house in Erie County. Built long before the advent of balloon framing, it is supported by concealed rough-hewn corner timbers. Among its interesting old features are its handsome carved doorway, lintels, and fireplaces, its marvelous wall stenciling, and its secret attic hideout. Another landmark of Griffin's Mills is the Presbyterian Church (1832). It has some Federal details similar to those of the Paul-McCormick house and a Greek Revival feeling as well. The former parsonage at 1693 Mill Road dates from 1834. There is evidence that the Bausch house, also Federal, situated just west of the Presbyterian Church, may date from about 1810, for a strong tradition exists that it sheltered refugees during the War of 1812. Griffin's Mills remains a quiet country street lined with buildings, over half of which date back to its period of tannery, mill, and distillery prosperity in the early nineteenth century.

The old Lake Shore Road southwest of Buffalo presents a variety of architectural charms, outstanding of which is "Graycliff," Darwin Martin's summer house at Derby (1927), by Frank Lloyd Wright. This structure and its outbuildings are now occupied by the Piarist Fathers.

Kenmore

1 **Eberhardt House, 1893–1894**
(now Jack Hunt—Coin Broker)
2746 Delaware Avenue at Kenmore Avenue
Architect: Cyrus K. Porter

This home and its twin next door, which was demolished in 1977, were built as examples of the type of housing that the Eberhardt brothers planned to develop throughout Kenmore, one of Buffalo's first suburban areas.

Town of Tonawanda

2 **Chevrolet Plant, 1937**
River Road
Architect: Albert Kahn

This long, low plant building permits straight-line assembly, necessary for the economical mass production of automobiles. In this respect the design represents an advance over the Pierce-Arrow complex (1906–1907), with which the Kahn firm was also associated.

City of Tonawanda

3 **New York Central Railway Station, 1870**
(now Historical Society of the Tonawandas Museum)
113 Main Street at Grove Street

4 **Benjamin Long Homestead, 1829**
24 East Niagara Street

This is the oldest building in the City of Tonawanda. It was restored in 1980 and is now open to the public.

Grand Island

5 **Lewis Allen House (Riverlea), 1840**
Beaver Island State Park

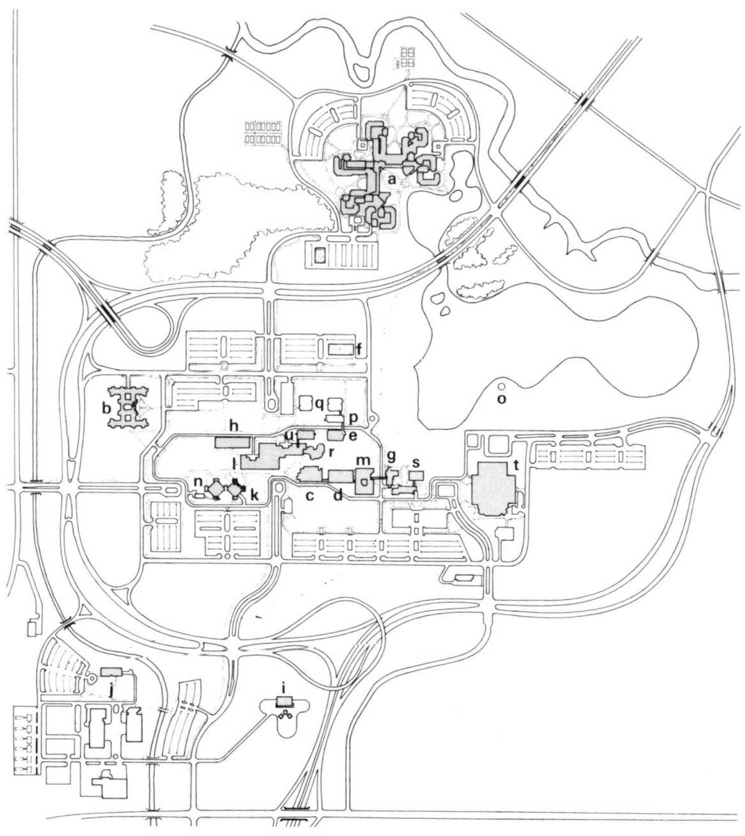

Amherst **6** **State University of New York at Amherst Campus**

The campus was developed on a 1200-acre site 3 miles north of the Main Street Campus after considerable debate at both state and local levels. Several alternative sites were proposed, including an extension to the Main Street Campus and a waterfront location near downtown Buffalo. The rejection of the waterfront site is still seen by many as a great lost opportunity for both the university and the city.

After 1958, when Nelson Rockefeller, then Governor of New York State, proposed to enlarge the State University of New York system, several alternative design proposals for Buffalo were proposed, including a megastructure by native son Gordon Bunshaft. The chosen master plan, 1970, was by Sasaki, Dawson and DeMay, of Watertown, Massachusetts. It has been greatly altered, particularly in the handling of exterior materials.

283
Erie County

a Ellicott Complex, Davis Brody and Associates

b Governor's Residence Halls, I. M. Pei

c O'Brian Hall, Harry Weese Associates

d Baldy Hall, Harry Weese Associates

e Bell Hall, Marcel Breuer Associates

f "The Bubble," Birdair Structures, Inc.

g Clemens Hall, Ulrich Franzen

h Fronczak Hall, Armand Bartos and Associates

i Chilled Water Plant, Davis Brody and Associates

j Crofts Administration and Service Building, Biggie-Shaflucas

k Cooke Towers and Hochstetter Towers, Hellmuth, Obata and Kassabaum

l Capen Hall, Sasaki, Dawson and DeMay

m Lockwood Library, Harry Weese Associates

n Dorsheimer Laboratory, William L. Long Associates

o Baird Point Open Air Amphitheater, Peter Castle

p Furnas Hall, Marcel Breuer

q East and West Engineering Buildings, Marcel Breuer

r East Lecture Halls, Hamilton, Houston, Lownie

s Baird Music Hall and Slee Chamber Hall, Ulrich Franzen

t Alumni Arena, Robert T. Coles

u Educational Communications Center, Hamilton, Houston, and Lownie

6a The Joseph Ellicott Complex, 1972–1975
State University of New York at Amherst
Architects: Davis, Brody and Associates; Milstein, Wittek, Davis and Associates (associated architects)

285
Erie County

The Joseph Ellicott complex was designed by Davis, Brody and Associates to provide 3200 resident students and 2700 commuters with classrooms, dining, recreational, theater, and other facilities integrated into a six-college residential scheme. The architects chose to strike a balance between extremes of height and lateral sprawl in designing this urbane megastructure. The core of the plan consists of a bus tunnel and a parallel pedestrian avenue which forms a right angle at the center. The six colleges, each one a U-shaped cluster surrounding a courtyard, are distributed two at each end of the core and two at the corner. The buildings vary in height from two stories at the core and plaza level to ten in some of the residential towers. The tallest towers are banked by lesser units so as to diminish their real height and enhance the picturesqueness of the whole complex.

The block-pile appearance of the complex stems from the architect's desire to have every change in internal spatial function be reflected on the outer surfaces of the buildings. Thus, cantilevered stories signal changes from semipublic dining and lounge spaces upward to undergraduate dormitory rooms, and further projections indicate shifts from undergraduate to graduate residences. Stair and elevator towers are visibly projected from the buildings as well. Dining, lounge, and pedestrian spaces are all characterized by unusually large windows, which provide visual contact with the world outside the walls. Unfortunately, the compelling romantic image of the complex is based upon its multiplicity of surfaces, each of which loses far more heat to the frigid winter air masses than would a more conventional design.

Williams-ville	7	**Williamsville Water Mills, 1811** 56 Spring Street The watermill, overlooking Glen Park, is the oldest continuously operating business in Erie County.
Akron	8	**Octagon House, 1849** Main Street and Parkview Drive Builder: Charles B. Rich This building was modeled on octagon houses first designed by Orson Fowler in the Hudson River area of New York.
Cheek-towaga	9	**Our Lady Help of Christians Chapel, 1853** (now Maria Hilf Chapel) 4125 Union Road Builder: Franz Joseph Batt Addition: 1871 Restored: 1975 National Register of Historic Places
Lancaster	10	**Town Hall Opera House, 1894** 10 Central Avenue Builder: George Metzger Restored: 1980

East Aurora 11 **Millard Fillmore Cottage, 1826**
24 Shearer Avenue
National Historic Landmark

Millard Fillmore resided here until 1830. The house was acquired by the Aurora Historical Society in 1975 and has been restored.

12 **Roycroft Campus, 1895 onward**
Main Street at South Grove Street
National Register of Historic Places

Here Elbert Hubbard established his arts and crafts community. He based it on the socially progressive ideas of William Morris, after he had visited Morris in England when writing his *Little Journeys to the Homes of the Great.*

Hubbard was the highly successful chief salesman and a partner in the Larkin Company in Buffalo until in 1893, at the age of 37, he gave it all up and went to Harvard to gain a formal education. The attempt was not a success and his restlessness and urge to write took him to England and Ireland to meet the men he admired and later wrote about in the *Little Journeys.* On his return he set up the Roycrofters at East Aurora, who, by early in the twentieth century, were already producing their famous solid, mission-style furniture. They also produced a considerable range of books and pamphlets which attracted visitors and craftsmen from all over the world.

All the main ''campus'' buildings survive, built in a variety of styles culminating in the bindery, a large shingle structure of considerable originality at the back of the site.

13 **Stephen Clement Estate Barn**
(now Barn Shoppe)
Mill at Beech Road

The enormous size of the barn is made possible by a steel-truss roof structure.

Wales

14 **Gail-Bleak House, circa 1837**
Route 78 in Wales Center, on the Strykersville Road outside East Aurora

The Gail-Bleak house has been called the finest Gothic Revival structure in Erie County.

15 **Griffin's Mills**
Route 240 at Mill Road

Lacka-wanna **16** **Our Lady of Victory Basilica, 1922–1926**
South Park Avenue at Ridge Road
Architect: Emile Uhlrich

Located just outside the City of Buffalo limits, the basilica is one of the most prominent landmarks in Lackawanna, second only to the Bethlehem Steel Mills. The exterior of this ornate baroque structure is clad in Georgia and Carrara marble and features twin towers 165 feet high capped by solid copper angels. The interior is especially noted for its rich use of materials, including different types of marble, as well as mahogany woodwork, and numerous fixtures of gold, silver, copper, and bronze.

Hamburg 17 **Lakeshore-Michigan Railroad Station, 1897**
Lakeside Cemetery between Camp and Rogers Roads

The railroad station was planned in conjunction with the former Buffalo World Cemetery, so that bodies could be easily transported from the city to countryside grave sites.

18 **Hamburg-Lakeview School, 1910**
(now Calvary Way Baptist School)
2095 Lakeview Road

This is an unusual vernacular wooden building distinguished by its keyhole motif.

19 **Health and Social Service Exhibition, 1885**
Erie County Fairgrounds

Besides the Rich House in Akron, this is the only other octagonal building in Erie County.

Derby 20

Graycliff, 1927
(former Darwin D. Martin summer home)
6472 Old Lakeshore Road
Architect: Frank Lloyd Wright

The Martin summer home, one of Frank Lloyd Wright's few commissions during the middle and late 1920s, is a testament to his warm and lasting friendship with Darwin D. Martin. Hitchcock found the house "clumsy in detail," but the design is of interest today for the way it is adjusted to its site high upon a cliff above Lake Erie. Wright seems to have considered every possible summer weather condition in this design. The long narrow plan and generous windows made it possible to channel lake breezes directly through all of the living and sleeping spaces. The lawn was dished out to a depth of about four feet in order to provide a pool of warm sunlight in the front yard, while the opposite side of the house featured a deeply shadowed terrace as a retreat from the sun on the hottest summer days. The L-shaped chimney opened broadly into the living room and toward the dining room as well. An early morning fire (servants were on hand) warmed a small bathroom that Wright placed *inside* the chimney mass on the floor above. This house was made for the enjoyment of natural things. Whatever its aesthetic shortcomings it gives us a glimpse into the mind of the Wright who would soon design the Fallingwater house and the Jacobs Solar Hemicycle. Graycliff has been considerably altered, although no major portion of the structure, including the garage, has been demolished.

Architecture in Niagara County, as elsewhere, parallels the economic and social history of the area. Particularly evident throughout the county is the farmhouse, in every style ranging from Federal to Queen Anne. Its prevalence is a reflection of the agricultural tradition of Niagara County, especially in the fruit belt along the Lake Ontario shore.

Unique in Niagara County are the half-timbered, clay structures erected by North German settlers in the 1840s. Wisconsin is the only other area in the United States where this type of construction exists in any abundance. In 1843, a group of north Germans migrated to America in search of religious freedom. They came to Niagara County because a group of fellow Lutherans had settled earlier in Buffalo. They purchased land in Wheatfield, Niagara, and Royalton and established the settlements of Bergholz, Walmore, St. Johnsburg, Martinsville, and Wolcottsville. A second migration occurred in 1857. Some members of these groups eventually emigrated to Wisconsin.

In Germany, Frederick the Great had ruled that only half-timbered structures could be built. Here, where wood was plentiful, this type of construction was unnecessary. But tradition prevailed. The structures were prefabricated. As timbers were cut and adzed, roman numerals and slashes were carved into the beams for easy assembly. Clay was gathered on site and mixed with straw, and the nogging applied between the timbers. Approximately twelve of these structures are known to survive in the county.

One of the particular delights of Niagara County is its cobblestone architecture. A combination of Ice Age geology, a farmers' nuisance, and unemployed masons from the Erie Canal led to this unique building method. Its prime period ranged from 1825 to the Civil War. Niagara County has approximately fifty cobblestone structures, the greatest number of which are in the Greek Revival style.

Probably the most influential event in determining the development of the county came in 1825 with the opening of the Erie Canal. All across the state, small communities grew up along the towpaths. These communities, such as Middleport, had a small-town grandeur which reflected the prosperity that the canal generated. Fortunately, even after the economic prosperity declined, these towns generally avoided the ''urban clearance'' programs that larger cities adopted and consequently preserved much of their architectural heritage.

Niagara Falls

Niagara Falls, a city with a natural wonder of the world, has experienced several cycles of prosperity and decline. Its first heyday came in the mid-nineteenth century with the advent of the railroads. A boom in hotels and related tourist establishments contributed to Niagara Falls's development as a thriving village. The 1890s brought the development of power and, as a consequence, much industrial growth. In 1892, Niagara Falls became a city. Another construction boom took place in the downtown area in 1925. Many of the original village structures were taken down at this time and replaced by new skyscrapers in the popular Art Deco style. The city continued to prosper until the 1960s, when the effects of universal urban changes weakened the central city. During this time urban renewal projects destroyed almost all the old structures of the south end area. In their place, the International Convention Center, the E. Dent Lackey Plaza, the Falls Street Mall and Wintergarden, and the Native American Center for the Living Arts (the Turtle) have been constructed, reflecting the attempt to stimulate a new era of prosperity through tourism.

Lewiston

Lewiston, located on the Niagara River at the foot of the Niagara Portage, became a direct line of transportation between the ocean and the upper Great Lakes. The French and English both used the portage route for their enterprises. The first permanent settlement was established in

1800. Taverns emerged along with dwellings. Hustler's Tavern and the Frontier House remain today, the former having been remodeled in the late nineteenth century and the latter having become a McDonald's restaurant, but with its original exterior.

Youngstown

Youngstown, one of the oldest villages on the Niagara Frontier, owes its existence to the settlement around Fort Niagara. It served as a port of entry beginning in 1799, because of its location at the mouth of the Niagara River. The main section of the fort, "the Castle," dates from 1726. Joncaire, a French trader, arranged with the Seneca Indians to have the trading post built. Some of the Main Street buildings in Youngstown date from the 1840s. Of particular note is the stone tavern, built in 1842. A beautiful example of church architecture is Richard Upjohn's St. John's Episcopal Church at the corner of Main and Chestnut. The 1878 structure was one of Upjohn's prefabricated models; the chalk numbers that guided assembly are barely visible on the walls and ceiling.

Lockport

Lockport's existence as a city is due to its location where the Erie Canal passed through the old lake shore ridge. A series of locks were constructed to make this transition. Settlers ready to take advantage of the prospect of growth soon found their way to the village. Within a matter of years, a booming community developed. Lowertown flourished around the canal because of the available water power. Mills, factories, and dwellings emerged in the late 1820s and 1830s. Manufacturing prospered, and by the 1860s, the elite had moved to Uppertown's magnificent houses. Most of these were constructed in a then popular Italianate style.

North Tonawanda

1 **Wilhelm House, 1843**
278 Old Falls Boulevard

This half-timber and clay structure is being restored by the Historical Society of North German Settlements in Western New York.

Niagara Falls

2 **Echota Planned Community, 1894**
A Street through F Street
Architects: McKim, Mead and White

The 84-acre development was originally designed to accommodate families of area industrial workers, who were housed in 67 structures designed by Stanford White, many of which have since been moved to the Veterans' Height project in the Town of Niagara. Amenities such as electric lights, running water, and kitchen sinks were included in the low-cost model housing, advanced for its time in these provisions.

3 **First Government Housing Project, 1918**
23rd, 24th and 25th Streets between Ferry and Orleans Avenue
Architect: Chester Wright

This project was designed to provide rental housing for workers at the area's defense industry plants.

4 **Adams Power Station #3, 1895**
1701 Buffalo Avenue
Architects: McKim, Mead and White
National Register of Historic Places

The world's first large-scale facility for the production of alternating electric current included this plant, the last remaining structure of a complex which originally covered an entire city block. Both George Westinghouse and Thomas Edison were deeply involved in the initial development.

5 **Whitney Mansion, circa 1830–1850**
335 Buffalo Avenue
National Register of Historic Places

A fine example of Greek Revival architecture, this stone house overlooks the rapids on the south side of Buffalo Avenue.

6 **Convention Center, 1971–1973**
305 Fourth Street
Architects: Johnson and Burgee

The arched construction of the Convention Center preserves the rainbow theme, so long a part of Niagara Falls imagery.

7 Wintergarden, 1975–1977
Rainbow Boulevard South at the Falls Street Mall
Architects: Gruen Associates

The Wintergarden was designed to connect the Convention Center with the park at the brink of Niagara Falls. It possesses a striking profile and exposed steel-frame structure.

8 Carborundum Center, 1972
345 Third Street at Niagara Street
Architect: Gordon Bunshaft for Skidmore, Owings and Merrill

---

9 **Earl W. Brydges Public Library, 1973–1974**
1425 Main Street
Architect: Paul Rudolph

The sculptural form of this building demonstrates Rudolph's work in one of his more expressionistic phases. In fact, the building has been more successful from an aesthetic than a functional standpoint. Alterations are proposed to correct problems related to the roofing system which would greatly modify the exterior appearance of the library.

10 **Hooker Company Building, 1980–1981**
Prospect Street near the Rainbow Bridge
Architect: Cannon Design, Inc.

The Hooker building is enclosed by two walls separated by a four-foot airspace, which reduces heat loss while permitting large amounts of glazing.

11 **DeVeaux School, 1853**
3100 Lewiston Road
National Register of Historic Places

An orphan asylum, military academy, and school for children with learning disabilities have all been housed in this structure, named for Samuel DeVeaux, a merchant whose bequest financed its construction. The Buscaglia-Castellani Art Gallery is now located in one of its buildings.

Lewiston

12 **Frontier House, 1824–1825**
(now McDonald's Restaurant)
450 Center Street
Builders: J. Fairbanks, B. Barton, and S. Barton
National Register of Historic Places

This structure was originally built as a stagecoach stop when Lewiston was part of the "great overland route" across the continent.

13 **Earl W. Brydges Artpark, 1973–1974**
Route 18F at Portage Road on the Niagara River
Architects: Hardy, Holzman and Pfeiffer

Artpark's site on the escarpment of the Niagara River provides a dramatic context for the buildings and environmental sculpture located here.

Youngs-town

14 **St. John's Episcopal Church, 1878**
Main Street at Chestnut Street
Architect: Richard Upjohn

This is a fine example of the Carpenter Gothic style.

15 **Fort Niagara, 1678**
Main Street near Jackson Street
National Register of Historic Places

Although the first buildings at Fort Niagara were constructed in 1678, the oldest remaining structure is "the Castle," a French chateau-style fortress which dates from 1726. A War of 1812 cemetery is also located on the grounds.

16 **Anchor Farm, 1844**
Towline Road (Route 425) near Ide Road

Ship captain Morgan Johnson built this cobblestone Greek Revival home.

Lockport

17 **Vine Street School, 1864**
Vine Street at Garden Street

This Italianate two-room schoolhouse is an unusually elaborate example of a simple building type.

18 **Washington Hunt House, 1831**
Market Street at North Adam

Flemish bond brickwork and carved stone lintels enhance the original structure, which was modified by the addition of a side porch, extended eaves, and cornice brackets in later years.

19 **Lockport Canal Museum (Old City Hall)**
Pine Street at Lock 34

Originally a flour mill, this stone structure served as Lockport's City Hall between 1893 and 1974. In addition to serving as headquarters for the Niagara County Canal Trail, it also houses a restaurant.

20 Canal Locks

The Erie Canal was completed in 1825 and enlarged for the first time in 1847. A double set of five-flight locks dates from this period, with a total lift capacity of fifty-six feet. Two additional locks were completed in 1918.

21 Kenan Center
433 Locust Street

Theater, art, and recreational facilities are housed at the 100-year-old Kenan Center, which includes a Victorian brick home and carriage house on the grounds.

22 Cobblestone House
5936 Robinson Road near Transit Road

11 Other Western New York Counties

In addition to Erie and Niagara Counties, six other counties—Orleans, Genesee, Wyoming, Allegany, Cattaraugus, and Chautauqua—are included in the architectural purview of this book. These eight westernmost counties of New York State, legislatively linked as the state's Eighth Judicial District, are commonly called Western New York. Together with southern Ontario, they possess a certain architectural homogeneity as well as outstanding examples of nineteenth-century styles. For example, in his *Greek Revival Architecture in America* (1944), Talbot Hamlin wrote, "Nowhere more than in upstate New York is . . . Greek Revival work more vital and more varied. . . . Whoever those designers and builders were, again and again, they built well, and the houses they put up do much to make the character of upper New York what it is." Similar comments could be made about the quality of other styles found in the Western New York area.

Throughout the region the architectural traveler finds a considerable variety of form and style—the vernacular, the classical, and the contemporary. Driving the rural backroads and the village streets will yield many pleasant surprises, as one comes upon solitary structures and groups of buildings that have been well kept and remain basically unaltered over the past century or more. The homesteads, farms, schoolhouses, and churches of the early settlers reflect the straightforwardness and austerity of the pioneering spirit. Some of these buildings also suggest the use of the pattern books, the changes in architectural fashions, and the forms of architecture that settlers brought with them from eastern New York and New England.

Interspersed with vernacular buildings are many imposing mansions of the local leadership in agriculture, merchandising, and industry. More than a few Western New York communities expected that because of their location on the Erie Canal, the lake shore, or the highways of the new frontier they would develop into the regional capital. The High Victorian mansions, particularly, reflect these dreams, which were dashed by economic changes and the emergence of Buffalo as the region's key community.

Although a number of Western New York communities and their buildings have remained relatively intact since the nineteenth century, others give evidence of the depredations of time and the inroads of an often dull or insensitive "modernization."

Orleans County

Orleans County is a Lake Ontario–Erie Canal county, and, like Niagara County, includes several nineteenth-century canal communities, such as Albion and Medina. Its old lake shore forms the historic ridge road to Niagara, the principal highway from time immemorial of the Iroquois Indian and of the early white man.

The finest architectural treasures in Orleans County are probably the intricate cobblestone structures which abound in this area. A number are located on or near Route 104 (the Old Ridge Road). The First Universalist Church (1834) at Childs and the old schoolhouse nearby are two outstanding examples of cobblestone art. Others can be found at Gaines, Lyndonville, and Millville. Albion also boasts several fine examples, as well as a number of landmark buildings included in the Historic American Buildings Survey: the Tousle-Church-D.A.R. House (cited by Talbot Hamlin), the First Presbyterian Church, and the Pratt Opera House.

Orleans County is directly linked to several of Buffalo's outstanding edifices, such as H. H. Richardson's Buffalo State Hospital and a half dozen of the city's handsomest churches along Delaware, Elmwood, and Richmond Avenues. The reddish brown Medina sandstone used in these structures was quarried in Orleans County.

Genesee County

It was from the Holland Land Company office in Batavia that Joseph Ellicott came about 1800 to the place where Buffalo Creek flowed into Lake Erie. Here he surveyed, planned, and founded what became the city of Buffalo. Genesee

County's architectural heritage is best seen in the qualities of Batavia's buildings, such as the Holland Land Company Offices Museum, the Genesee County Courthouse, and the Richmond Memorial Library, the Batavia Club (now Bank of Genesee), the Alexander Classical School (now Town Hall Museum) and the Four Corners Historic District.

Wyoming County

One can best experience Wyoming County's great variety of stylistic forms by driving leisurely through its many villages, which have remained virtually unchanged since the last century. Notable structures are the Van Arsdale house and the Baptist church in Castile, the Richard Upjohn Carpenter Gothic board-and-batten church and the Masonic Temple in Warsaw, and the Greek Revival (1817) Middlebury Academy Museum in the village of Wyoming.

"Glen Iris," the former Letchworth mansion, which stands in Letchworth State Park on the Genesee River, has become a charming inn, still furnished with Letchworth family antiques, a delightful place to dine or lodge within sight and sound of the park's most spectacular waterfall.

Allegany County

Like Wyoming County, much of Allegany County has survived "modernization" well. Indeed, it is one of New York State's most rural counties. One finds on the campus of Alfred University a small but carefully crafted and highly ornamented building called "Terra Cotta," an early twentieth-century product of the university's ceramics department. Also on the Alfred campus stands "the Steinham," a delicately framed, small stone castle, overlooking one of Allegany County's picturesque mountainsides. Adjoining it is the nation's finest carillon of seventeenth-century Dutch bells.

Allegany also prides itself on the gracious, nearly intact Village Circle buildings of Angelica's Historical District, where, as in the villages of Wyoming County, automobiles look out of place. Angelica takes its name from Angelica Schuyler, the wife of John B. Church, who acquired 100,000 acres of land in the Genesee Valley. She thus became the first mistress of "Belvidere," just west of Belmont, a Federal brick house built about 1807 on the Church estate overlooking the Genesee River. Belvidere is reputed to have been designed by Benjamin Latrobe, architect of the original U.S. Capitol.

Cattaraugus County

The early history of Cattaraugus County is recorded at the Seneca-Iroquois National Museum, West of Salamanca. In this county one also finds the nation's largest state park, Allegany State Park.

Chautauqua County

Perhaps the best known and most architecturally documented Western New York county is Chautauqua. Its national renown stems principally from the Chautauqua Institute at Chautauqua. It has been a wide-ranging, philosophical-cultural enterprise on the shore of beautiful Lake Chautauqua for more than a century. One discovers set close together on quaint little streets within the grounds of the institute a picturesque assemblage of charming buildings, dating from 1874.

Ashville and Panama offer a number of outstanding and well-kept Greek Revival houses. Two in Ashville are the Smith-Bly-Fancher House (circa 1835) and the Atherly-Swanson House, built a little later.

Fredonia includes buildings by I. M. Pei on the campus of the State University College at Fredonia, as well as many outstanding examples of nineteenth-century architecture. In Westfield the McClurg mansion and the Rynd-Poletto house (circa 1867) are of interest.

Jamestown's architecture encompasses the palatial Italianate Governor Fenton House (Historical Society Museum), and a warm, Richardson-inspired library. Along with its older residential and downtown precinct, Jamestown has much to offer.

Finally, one cannot help noticing the many signs of revitalization in these Western New York areas. Along with the increased awareness of their fine architectural heritage, these communities are restoring, rehabilitating, and planning for a future environment which will utilize and highlight their treasury of good buildings.

Just across the Niagara River from Buffalo lies the Canadian province of Ontario. Its architecture is closely linked with that on the American side, since both cultures share a common English heritage. A less well-known reason for the architectural similarity is that after the Revolutionary War, Great Britain gave land in Canada to United Empire Loyalists (known as Tories in the United States), many of whom settled near the border. The houses they built resemble those they left behind in New England, New York, and Pennsylvania.

Superb examples of these houses are found in the beautifully maintained village of Niagara-on-the-Lake, across the Niagara River from Fort Niagara, where the river flows into Lake Ontario. Niagara-on-the-Lake looks like a late-eighteenth-century New England village lifted bodily and put down on the Canadian shore of Lake Ontario. The village was founded by about 200 veterans of the Loyalist regiment known as Butler's Rangers. Under Lieutenant Colonel John Butler these American colonists had fought for Britain against the American rebels from 1777 to 1784. In return the British government gave them land in Canada.

Originally called Newark, Niagara-on-the-Lake served as the first capital of Upper Canada (now Ontario) from 1792 to 1796, when Lieutenant Governor John Simcoe, for safety reasons, moved the capital to York (now Toronto). During the War of 1812 American forces burned the village (the British retaliated by burning the village of Buffalo), but Niagara-on-the-Lake soon rose again almost in its original form. The houses, under towering trees, are mostly in Federal or modest cottage styles. Brick and wooden houses alike have fine fanlighted doorways and superb interior details. The shops along Queen Street and several inns, the Angel Inn (1823), the Oban Inn (1824), the Prince of Wales Hotel (1864), and the Pillar and Post (1911) have been well restored.

When the Welland Canal opened in the 1830s, the main trade route up the lakes bypassed Niagara-on-the-Lake, and it became a summer resort area and eventually the home of the prestigious Shaw Festival and Theater. But the village is still linked to the past through its historic buildings and nearby Fort George.

Moving south along the Niagara Parkway overlooking the Niagara River gorge, one comes to Queenston, scene of the War of 1812 Battle of Queenston Heights, where British General Isaac Brock was killed. His monument dominates the landscape. Nearby are two distinguished old brick houses: the Fields house (circa 1800) in a southern-looking Federal style, one of the oldest brick dwellings in Ontario, and the Federal-style McFarland house, used as a hospital during the 1812 battle and now furnished in early nineteenth-century style. A few miles on is the Swartze House, also on the Niagara Parkway, and, like the Fields House, built by one of Butler's Rangers. A short distance away is the imposing Greek Revival mansion "Willowbank" (1832–1835). Queenston also possesses the fine restored stone Federal house occupied by William Lyon MacKenzie when he was editing the *Colonial Advocate* here in 1826, and the neat restored Laura Secord cottage (circa 1810). Her husband, too, was one of Butler's Rangers. Others of Butler's men were among the first to settle (in the early 1780s) in nearby St. Davids.

Continuing south above the Niagara River, one enters Niagara Falls, Ontario, where stood "Clifton" (1855–1860), one of the few Italianate houses designed by Richard Upjohn. All that survives is the carriage house, which forms part of the rear section of the Park Motor Hotel on Clifton Hill. Here also is Oak Hall Estate, the stone Gothic mansion built by millionaire Sir Harry Oakes, commanding a spectacular view of the Niagara Rapids.

Moving south again on the Niagara Parkway, one comes to Chippawa, scene of an American victory in the War of 1812. Here, where the Chippawa Creek flows into the Niagara River, stands Willoughby Hall, an imposing brick Neo-Georgian mansion built in 1845 by James Cummings on lands awarded his father Thomas, another of Butler's Rangers. A little farther on is Navy Island, site of Canadian William Lyon Mackenzie's provisional rebel government headquarters during the Patriots' Rebellion of 1837, and now a bird sanctuary and game preserve.

The Town of Fort Erie, just across the Peace Bridge from Buffalo, takes its name from the old fort built in the eighteenth century to command the entrance to the Niagara River and the trade route up the Great Lakes. Damaged in the War of 1812 and eroded by time, it was restored in 1939 and opened to the public. The settling of the Town of Fort Erie, like that of Niagara-on-the-Lake, owes much to United Empire Loyalists who were awarded land grants here. One of them was Abraham Wintemute, who, with his six sons, fought with Butler's Rangers. His house (circa 1800), now 487 Niagara Boulevard near Gilmore Road, still stands by the river. It is one of the oldest structures on either side of the river, and its Federal configuration is still discernible despite many alterations. A little to the north on Niagara Boulevard stands one of Canada's oldest brick Greek Revival houses, Bertie Hall, named after Lord Bertie, the King's representative in the Niagara area during the early nineteenth century. It was begun in about 1830 by two brothers, Brock and Nelson Forsyth, who were rumored to have made their money smuggling. Reputedly, it was a station on the Underground Railroad, sheltering fugitive slaves during the Civil War. It stands on land deeded by the Crown in 1806 to Henry Anguish, still another of Butler's Rangers. The Grange (circa 1836), so called because it was originally the rectory for old St. Paul's Church in Fort Erie, is beautifully situated at the end of a tree-lined lane at 1 Burns Place.

About two miles west from the Peace Bridge on Garrison Road (Route 3) stands one of the fine brick farmhouses indigenous to this area—the Cruikshank house (1850s). The kitchen section is older. This design became a familiar silhouette throughout Ontario—a two-story, side-gabled house, often of brick or stucco with a three- or five-bay elevation, a center doorway, a veranda, and a steeply peaked gable over the center opening. On a private dirt road off the Windmill Point Road near Lake Erie nestles a similar fine brick farmhouse with both Gothic Revival and Italianate detailing, the Graham house.

Occasionally one finds local limestone used as a building material, from quarries at Windmill Point and Sherkston. A fine example is the Lawson House at Prospect Point in Yacht Harbor, east of Crystal Beach. Built in 1812, it billeted British officers in the War of 1812 and sheltered two American fugitives from the Fenian Raid at the close of the Civil War. It has massive stone walls with built-in chimneys in the side gables and huge corner and floor-supporting beams. Other notable native limestone buildings in the area are the district schoolhouses—honest, solidly made vernacular buildings, front-gabled and well-proportioned with round-topped windows. Two near the Peace Bridge are number 4 on Garrison Road and number 5 on Dominion Road (both circa 1870). Somewhat earlier is the small Gothic Revival center section of the present Church of Christ (Disciples) on Stonemill Road near Dominion Road. The interior has been rebuilt. Stonemill Road is named after the old mill (circa 1830), which once stood on the lake shore.

Architectural Biographies

Frank Lloyd Wright's Buffalo Architecture

One of Frank Lloyd Wright's significant contributions to American architecture is the prairie house, a low-slung, open-planned structure designed to embrace nature and to conform to the flat midwestern landscape. Wright established the principles of the prairie style during his first decade of independent practice, between 1893 and 1903, and in the following decade he refined his ideas in numerous variations upon the theme. Most of the masterpieces of the prairie style are located in the vicinity of Chicago, where Wright practiced, but an outstanding exception is the Darwin D. Martin house in Buffalo, one of the most expensive and elaborate of all of the prairie houses. Darwin Martin, an officer of the highly successful Larkin Company, discovered Wright's work though his brother, William E. Martin, who had commissioned Wright to design a house in Oak Park, Illinois, in 1903. Darwin Martin persuaded Wright to do the complex of buildings at 125 Jewett Parkway and arranged to have him design the Larkin Administration Building shortly afterward. Two other Larkin executives, William R. Heath and Walter V. Davidson, also commissioned houses from Frank Lloyd Wright in 1905 and 1908, respectively. As a group the five extant Wright houses in Buffalo provide a unique opportunity, outside the Chicago area, to examine Wright's application of his organic and prairie principles to commissions which range from the extreme modesty of the gardener's cottage in the Martin complex to the intermediate scale of the Davidson house and on to the elaborate splendor of the Martin house.

Lockwood, Greene & Company

Lockwood, Greene & Company of Boston, Massachusetts (later Lockwood, Greene, Engineers, of New York and Spartanburg), was an all-round engineering and factory-design office with roots that go back to the middle of the nineteenth century. Originally specializing in textile mills, it expanded its business southward in step with the textile industry and, at the same time, moved into reinforced concrete construction, following the lead established by Ernest L. Ransome's United Shoe Machinery plant of 1906 at Beverly, Massachusetts.

Buffalo is fortunate that its golden age of industrial building coincided with the very best period of Lockwood, Greene's work in concrete: Graphic Controls (formerly Larkin Company), dating from 1911, is their first masterpiece in concrete. Bethune Hall (formerly Buffalo Meter Company), of 1915, already shows their design on the edge of self-conscious stylishness and decadence.

R. J. Reidpath and Son

Together with Bethune, Bethune and Fuchs, the Reidpath office was responsible for most of the better-designed early industrial architecture in Buffalo, and it was in its time the most productive and consistently excellent architectural office in the city. Although the business was closed down only in 1926 by Robert Reidpath's son (born in East Aurora and therefore christened Elbert Hubbard Reidpath after the local writer and artist), one can distinguish the father's hand as early as the date of the exteriors at the back of the original Larkin plant, from before 1885. The Reidpaths' great period was between 1900 and 1914, when they did all their work on the main Larkin complex and acted as structural engineers for the Martin house. The firm's masterpiece is undoubtedly the Alling and Cory warehouse of 1910 at Elm and North Division. Although it did a certain amount of work outside the United States, its main claim to international reputation must be that its one major grain elevator, the Dakota, was illustrated in 1913 in Walter Gropius's epoch-making article entitled "The Development of Modern Industrial Architecture."

Green and Wicks

Edward B. Green (1855–1950) and William Sydney Wicks (1854–1919) ran the leading architectural firm in Buffalo at the turn of the century. The partnership was originally established in Auburn, New York, shortly after Wicks's graduation from MIT. In addition to designing commercial buildings, the firm was much sought after by Buffalo society for private residences. It designed a number of mansions on Delaware Avenue and at other desirable addresses in Buffalo. After Wicks's death, the firm of Edward B. Green and Son was founded, and continued in practice until the death of Edward B. Green, Jr., in 1931. The firm became Green and James in 1936 and Green, James and Meadows in 1945.

George Cary

Cary was one of the few native-born architects in the city. He had spent a brief apprenticeship with McKim, Mead and White before going to study at the Ecole des Beaux-Arts in Paris (1886–1889). In 1891 he returned to Buffalo and set up practice. Marriage to Althea Birge, daughter of the president of the Pierce-Arrow Motor Car Company, coupled wealth to his old New England family background and assured his entry into the upper reaches of Buffalo society. Well-mannered and correct, Cary's architecture is less imaginative than that of Green and Wicks. He designed a number of homes and institutional structures, but he is best known for the Buffalo and Erie County Historical Society Building and the Pierce-Arrow Administration Building.

Esenwein and Johnson

After Green and Wicks, Esenwein and Johnson enjoyed the most active architectural practice in Buffalo at the turn of the century. August Carl Esenwein (1856–1926), the senior member of the firm, was born in Württemberg, in Germany, studied in Stuttgart, and worked in Paris before coming to Buffalo in 1880. James A. Johnson (1865–1939) had been an assistant in the office of McKim, Mead and White before joining Esenwein and made ornament his specialty. The motifs featuring electric motors and generators that decorate the exterior of the Niagara Mohawk Building—curious precursors of Art Deco ornamentation—were of his invention.

Chronological Table

	General Historical Data
1664	King Charles II grants the territory including the present-day city of Buffalo to James, Duke of York.
1669	The French explorer Robert Cavelier Sieur de La Salle builds his ship Griffon on the Niagara River opposite Cayuga Island.
1678	The first buildings at Fort Niagara, then called Fort Conti, are erected by the French in order to protect their supply routes over the Great Lakes.
1679	Father Louis Hennepin is the first white man to visit Niagara Falls.
1683	New York is established as a British colony.
1759	British capture Fort Niagara.
1775–1781	The American Revolution; the Treaty of Paris, 1783, defines the Niagara River as the boundary between British and United States territory.
1793	The Holland Land Company purchases 1½ million acres of land in Western New York; additional lands are bought from the Seneca Indians in 1797, excluding the Mile Strip reservation area along the Niagara River.
1794	Withdrawal of the British from Western New York territory is required by the terms of the Jay Treaty. (British troops evacuate Fort Niagara in 1796.)
1802	State Legislature extinguishes Seneca Indian title to the Mile Strip, and begins to plat and sell land to settlers in the Village of Black Rock area.
1810	Township of Buffalo is established, including New Amsterdam and Black Rock.
1812–1815	War of 1812; Buffalo is burned to the ground on New Year's Eve, 1813, in retaliation for the burning of Newark (now Niagara on the Lake), Ontario.
1813	Village of Buffalo is incorporated.
1817	Turnpike from Buffalo to Albany is completed; Erie Canal construction is begun.

Architectural/Planning Events

1726	"The Castle," Fort Niagara
1802–1805	Black Rock plan
1804	Joseph Ellicott, agent for the Holland Land Company, completes his plan for the Village of New Amsterdam.
c. 1808	Bowmansville cabin, the oldest extant structure in Erie County.
c. 1818	Coit house, the oldest extant structure in Buffalo.

Chronological Table (cont.)

	General Historical Data
1820	Population of the village of Buffalo: 2,095
1821	Erie County is established.
1825	Erie Canal is completed; Buffalo's growth as a major port begins.
1830	Population of the village of Buffalo: 8,668
1832	Buffalo is incorporated as a city.
1837	Nationwide financial panic; Benjamin Rathbun, Buffalo's major real estate developer and builder, is bankrupt.
1840	City population: 18,213
1842	Buffalo connected to Albany by rail.
1850	City population: 42,261 Millard Fillmore, a Buffalonian, becomes president upon the death of Zachary Taylor.
1853	Buffalo's boundaries are expanded to include 41 square miles.
1859	The Buffalo Street Railway, horse-drawn, begins operation.
1860	City population: 81,129
1861–1865	Civil War
1873	International Railroad Bridge is constructed; nationwide financial panic.
1880	City population: 155,134
1882	Grover Cleveland is elected mayor of Buffalo; later becomes governor of New York State and in 1885 President of the United States.
1883	Lackawanna Railroad is constructed; the Central Wharf is demolished in the process; the Belt Line commuter railroad begins operation.
1890	City population: 255,664
1891	Streetcar service introduced on Niagara Street.

Architectural/Planning Events

1825	Frontier House
1826	Millard Fillmore house
1833	Buffalo Lighthouse First Unitarian Church
1838	Wilcox house
1842	Evans Elevator
1849–1851	St. Paul's Episcopal Cathedral
1868	Frederick Law Olmsted is commissioned to design Buffalo's park and parkway system.
1870–1896	Buffalo State Hospital
1871–1876	City and County Hall
1882–1896	McKim, Mead and White in Buffalo: Metcalfe house, Root house, G. Williams house, C. Williams house

Chronological Table (cont.)

	General Historical Data
1896	Electric power is transmitted from Niagara Falls to Buffalo.
1899	Lackawanna Iron and Steel Company is founded; heavy industry begins to replace commerce as the basis of the local economy.
1900	City population: 352,387, 69% of SMSA* total; Buffalo ranks as the eighth largest city in the U.S., and the sixth busiest fresh water port in the world.
1901	Pan-American Exposition is held at Buffalo; President William McKinley is assassinated while in attendance, and Theodore Roosevelt is sworn in as President at the Wilcox Mansion.
1910	City population: 495,453, 80% of SMSA total
1917–1918	U.S. enters World War I.
1920	City population: 506,775, 67% of SMSA total
1927	Peace Bridge to Canada is constructed.
1929–1933	Great Depression
1930	City population: 573,076, 63% of SMSA total
1940	City population: 575,901, 60% of SMSA total
1941–1945	U.S. enters World War II.
1950	City population: 580,132, 53% of SMSA total
1950–1953	U.S. enters Korean War.
1954–1959	St. Lawrence Seaway is constructed.
1960	City population: 532,759, 41% of SMSA total
1963–1973	U.S. enters Vietnam War.
1970	City population: 462,768, 34% of SMSA total. Buffalo ranks as the twenty-eighth largest city in the U.S.
1980	City population: 350,000, 30% of SMSA total; Buffalo is the thirty-seventh largest city in the U.S.

*Standard Metropolitan Statistical Area.

	Architectural/Planning Events
1895–1896	Prudential (Guaranty) Building Ellicott Square Building
1903–1908	Frank Lloyd Wright in Buffalo: Darwin D. Martin complex; Larkin Administration Building; Davidson house; Heath house
1906	Pierce-Arrow complex
1907	Daniel Burnham's plan for Niagara Square
1918	City Planning Committee established.
1929–1931	City Hall
1937	Chevrolet Plant
1938–1940	Kleinhans Music Hall
1950	Larkin Administration Building demolished.
1964–1974	Downtown urban renewal: M&T Bank, Marine Midland Bank, Main Place Mall, Shoreline Apartments
1975–1980	National Historic Districts declared: Delaware, Allentown, West Village. Main Street light rail rapid transit: waterfront redevelopment; entertainment district; Main-Genesee development

Selected Bibliography

Buffalo and Western New York History

Bingham, Robert Warwick. *The Cradle of the Queen City: A History to the Incorporation of the City.* Buffalo Historical Society Publication, vol. 31. Buffalo, 1931.

Bingham, Robert W., ed. *Holland Land Company Papers: Reports of Joseph Ellicott.* Buffalo Historical Society Publication, vols. 32 and 33. Buffalo, 1937.

Chazenoff, William. *Joseph Ellicott and the Holland Land Company.* Syracuse: Syracuse University Press, 1970.

Dunn, Walter S., Jr., ed. *History of Erie County, 1870–1970.* Buffalo: Buffalo and Erie County Historical Society, 1972.

Grendel, Stephen. *People of Our City and County* (Adventures in Western New York History Series). Buffalo: Buffalo and Erie County Historical Society, 1970.

Horton, John T.; Williams, Edward T.; and Douglas, Harry S. *History of Northwestern New York,* vols. 1 and 2. New York: Lewis Historical Publishing Company, 1947.

Smith, H. Perry. *History of the City of Buffalo and Erie County,* vols. 1 and 2. Syracuse: P. Mason & Company, 1884.

Welch, Samuel M. *Recollections of Buffalo: During the Decade from 1830 to 1840.* Buffalo: Peter Paul & Bro., 1891.

Buffalo and Western New York Architecture

Banham, Reyner. "Buffalo Industrial," *Little Journal*, vol. 3, no. 1. Society of Architectural Historians, Western New York Chapter, Feb. 1979.

———. "Buffalo Archaeological," *Architectural Review,* February 1980.

Conover, Jewel Helen. *Nineteenth Century Houses in Western New York.* Albany: State University of New York Press, 1966.

Fancher, Pauline. *Chautauqua, Its Architecture and Its People.* Miami: Banyon Books, 1978.

Fox, Austin M. Series of articles on Buffalo architecture, *Spree* magazine, fall 1980–fall 1981.

———. "Frank Lloyd Wright: His Buffalo Houses Revisited," *Spree,* fall 1979.

———. "The Mansard Style: How a French Law Created an Architectural Style," *Spree*, winter 1979.

———. "The Old Farm Homesteads of Buffalo: A Trip Through a Ray Bradbury Time Warp," *Spree*, spring 1980.

Grieves, Robert T. "Prudential," *Spree*, spring 1978.

Hamlin, Talbot. *Greek Revival Architecture in America.* New York: Dover Publications, 1964 (originally published in 1944).

Hamilton, Virginia, ed. *Aurora's Architectural Heritage.* East Aurora, N.Y.: East Aurora Historical Society, 1973.

Headrick, Maggie, and Ehrlich, Celia. *Seeing Buffalo*. Buffalo: Ivyhall, 1978.

Hitchcock, Henry-Russell, Jr. "Buffalo Architecture 1816–1940" (exhibition catalogue, unpublished). Buffalo: Albright Art Gallery, 1940.

Hubbell, Mark H., ed. *Beautiful Homes of Buffalo.* Buffalo: The Buffalo Truth Publishing Co., 1915.

———. *Beautiful Homes of Buffalo.* Buffalo: The Buffalo Truth Publishing Co., 1931.

Huxtable, Ada Louise. ''Writer Uncovers Pearls of Architecture among Urban Blight,'' *New York Times, Buffalo Courier Express*, Oct. 2, 1977.

Kowsky, Francis R. ''H. H. Richardson's Project for the Young Men's Association Library in Buffalo,'' *Niagara Frontier*, vol. 25, No. 2, 1978.

———. ''The William Dorsheimer House: A Reflection of French Suburban Architecture in the Early Work of H. H. Richardson.'' *The Art Bulletin.* Vol. 62, No. 1, March 1980.

———. ''Buffalo Projects: H. H. Richardson'' (exhibition catalogue). Buffalo State College Foundation, Inc., Nov. 1980.

———. ''A Building in the 'Early Colonial' Style by McKim, Mead and White,'' *Little Journal,* vol. 4, no. 1. Society of Architectural Historians, Western New York Chapter, Nov. 1980.

Randall, John D. *Buffalo and Western New York Architecture and Human Values.* Buffalo: Artcraft-Burow, 1976.

———. *Prudential Building.* Buffalo: Greater Buffalo Development Foundation, 1980.

———. ''Some Aspects of the Creativity of Sullivan and Wright,'' *Little Journal,* vol. 4, no. 1, Society of Architectural Historians, Western New York chapter, Nov. 1980.

Reiff, Daniel D. *Architecture in Fredonia, 1811–1972* (exhibition catalogue). Buffalo: Thorner-Sidney Press, 1972.

Roth, Leland M. ''Three Industrial Towns by McKim, Mead and White,'' *Journal of the Society of Architectural Historians*, vol. 38, no. 4, Dec. 1979.

Severance, Frank H. *The Picture Book of Earlier Buffalo.* Buffalo Historical Society Publication, vol. 16. Buffalo, 1912.

Shelgren, Olaf William, Jr.; Lattin, Cary; and Frash, Robert W. *Cobblestone Landmarks of New York State.* Syracuse: Syracuse University Press, 1978.

Shelgren, Olaf William, Jr. *Buffalo Homes* (Adventures in Western New York History Series). Buffalo: Buffalo and Erie County Historical Society, 1970.

Suozzi, Paul. *Three Walks Around and About Allentown.* Buffalo: Landmark Society of the Niagara Frontier, circa 1974.

Credits

In addition to the authors listed on the title page, the following individuals and organizations contributed material to the guidebook:

Project Coordinators
Mary Banham
Kathryn Carroll

Editorial Advisor
Jason Aronoff

Researchers
Daniel Kocieniewski
Donald Theurer

Map Maker
Frederick Zonsius

Administrative Assistant
Judith Hourihan

Photography and Illustrations:

Albright-Knox Art Gallery: pages 27, 28, 33, 169 upper, 222 upper

Jay Baxtresser: page 36 upper

Patricia Layman Bazelon: pages 8, 9, 22 lower, 43, 48, 54, 58, 62, 63, 69, 71, 75, 76, 78, 79, 86 lower, 88 upper, 90, 92 upper, 95 lower, 97, 101, 102 lower, 108, 110 upper, 112 middle, 114, 118, 120, 122 lower, 125, 126, 134, 141, 143, 145, 146, 148, 149 lower, 153, 154, 155, 157, 158, 159, 165 lower, 166 upper, 169 lower, 173, 175, 179 upper, 183, 184 upper, 185, 186, 187, 189 upper, 191, 201 upper, 204, 207 upper, 208, 210, 212, 217, 218, 220, 226, 227, 229, 242, 243, 247, 250, 251, 254 upper, 260 upper

Jack Boucher (Historic American Buildings Survey): pages v, 67 upper and lower, 83, 130, 166 lower, 167 upper

Buffalo and Erie County Historical Society: pages 4, 16, 20, 22 upper, 31, 32 upper, 46, 66, 82, 92 lower, 152, 156, 189 lower, 197 upper, 222 lower, 232, 254 lower, 266, 267, 272, 274, 275

Buffalo News: page 161 lower

William Clarkson (donor): pages 13 upper, 269, 270

Columbia University (Archive of Catalan Art and Architecture): pages 56 lower, 234 lower

Charles Duffy: pages 150 lower, 246

David Gordon: pages 163, 196

Hare Photographs Inc.: pages 94, 112 upper and lower, 137, 236 lower, 290

Joseph Hryvniak: pages 2, 36 lower, 73

Louis Jacobs and Cheryl Wendelken: page 256

Stephen Mangione: pages 13 lower, 59, 60 upper, 61, 64, 74, 77, 80, 85 upper, 86 upper, 95 upper, 102 upper, 110 lower, 111, 116, 117, 122 upper, 123, 124, 127, 131, 132, 136, 138, 147, 150 upper, 151 upper, 160, 171, 178, 179 lower, 180, 181, 182, 184 lower, 195, 199, 200, 201 lower, 202, 203, 209, 221, 223, 233, 234 upper, 236 upper, 238, 239, 240, 241, 244, 259, 260 lower, 261, 286, 287, 288, 289, 291, 297 upper, 298, 299, 300, 301, 302, 303

Myers Studios Inc.: page 237

Paul Pasquarello: page 56 upper, 60 lower, 165 upper, 197 lower, 206, 207 lower, 297 lower

John D. Randall (donor): page 67 middle

State University of New York at Buffalo: page 284

Donald Theurer: pages 129, 149 upper, 161 upper, 219

Ronald Thomas: page 85 lower

Don Weigel Studio: page 254 middle

The following people also assisted in the preparation of the guidebook: Gail Amigone, Maureen Burgio, Edna Carroll, George Collins, Dennis Francis, Janice Gallivan, Kathryn Greenthal, Suzanne Johnson, Henry LaFarge, Sarah Landau, Joseph Lienert, Deborah Mattice, William Olaf Shelgren, Jr., Irene Simon-Sipos, Jennifer Tresch, H. Barbara Weinberg, Richard Guy Wilson.

Index